With all good wishes

אני.ב.ל

Herman Taube

BETWEEN THE SHADOWS

Books by Herman Taube

The Unforgettable
Remember (with Susan Taube)
Empty Pews
The Last Train
The Refugees
Red Village
A Chain of Images
Echoes
Questions
We Are Here

BETWEEN THE SHADOWS

new and selected works by
HERMAN TAUBE

foreword by
ELIE WIESEL

watercolors by
STEFFI RUBIN

DRYAD PRESS
JEWISH FOLK ARTS SOCIETY

Many of the poems in this collection originally appeared in
periodicals, including *The American University Magazine, Journal
of Jewish Communal Service, University of Maryland Koach
Magazine, The New American, The Washington Jewish Week, The
Jewish Times, HaYotzer, Algemeiner Journal, Rescue and
Resistance, Yom Tov Bletter-Johannesburg, Yiddishe Tzaitung,
Letzte Nayes-Israel, The Voice of Combatants and Partisans,
HaDoar, The View from the Top of the Mountain, The Barnwood
Press Anthology, Novo Momento-Sao Paulo, Illustrirte Bletter,
Anthology of Jewish Resistance, Memorial Book of the World
Gathering of Holocaust Survivors* and *Forward.* Also included in
this volume are poems published in the author's previous books: *A
Chain of Images, Echoes, Questions, We Are Here.*

This project is supported by a grant to Dryad Press from the
National Endowment for the Arts, a Federal agency.

The author would like to thank Joseph Mendelsohn and Sam H.
Miller for their generous support and Merrill Leffler and Mark
Esterman for their help in preparing this collection for publication.

Library of Congress Cataloging in Publicatons Data
Taube, Herman.
    Between the Shadows.
        1. Holocaust, Jewish (1939-1945) — Poetry. I. Title.
PS357-.A86B4   1985   811'.54   85-13005
ISBN 0-931848-71-7
ISBN 0-931848-72-5 (pbk.)

DRYAD PRESS
15 SHERMAN AVENUE
TAKOMA PARK, MARYLAND 20912

P.O. BOX 2916 PRESIDIO
SAN FRANCISCO, CALIFORNIA 94123

JEWISH FOLK ARTS SOCIETY
11710 HUNTERS LANE
ROCKVILLE, MARYLAND 20852

To my friends
Martha and Joseph Mendelsohn

Contents

Journey Back

Poland   3
Evacuation   5
Evacuation — II   7
Cherniachow   9
Never Again Will I Blame God   11
A Soldier and A Dog   12
Vodka   14
Last Hour in Majdanek   16
Monuments   19
Warsaw   20
Warsaw   21
The Stone   22
Suitcases. . .   24
Avremel the Tailor   25
Yankel Wassertreger   27
A Single Hair   28
Rabbi Moses Isserles O'H   31
Rabbi Yehudah Ajzenberg Z"L   33
On a Journey Back Home   35
Henoch. . .   36
My Girlfriend. . .   38
Way Home   40
Zawadzka 29,   41
The Messiah Came to Europe   43
The Chosen People   44
The Struma   45
Numbers   46
A Lonely Bird   48

Darkest Light

Letter to a Poet   51
Together   52
Silence   53
Hilda Thieberger   54
Contradiction   55
The Only Jew in Town   57
Encounter with a Rocking Chair   59
March 10,   60

A Survivor's Husband   61
Visiting a Home in Sao Paulo   63
Letter to a Survivor   65
On Vacation   66
California Condors   67
Encounter with a Friend   68
Insects Won the Battle   70
Self Portrait   71
I Am a Poet   73
The Centerpiece   74
Sadness Looks from Your Face   75
Abraham Sutzkever   77
Janusz Korchak   79
Your Junk Man   81
Images   82
To the Image in the Mirror   84
Two Stones   88
A Fourteenth Street Personage   90
Holes in a Pot   91
Yoachimowicz   92
Who Am I?   93
To Judy   95
Confidence   96
Spring   97
Zechariah Came to Brooklyn. . .   98
I Am a Dandelion   100

Living Shadows

Tashlich   105
Nei'lah   106
Yom Kippur Eve in a Temple   108
A Visit to a Friend's Sukkah   110
Hoshana Rabba   112
On the Other Hand   114
Yiddish   116
Maoz Tzur   118
Monologue by a Lonely Man. . .   119
I Feel Guilty. . . .   120
What Is Torah?   121
Playing Games   123

A Common Man In Search of G-d   124
From Doubt to Faith   127
Friday Sunset   128
A Vision   129
A Prayer   130
Realization   131
Chrabrost-Courage!   132
Teachers   135
Poetic Notes   136

Mirror of Memory

The Grocer on Warner Street   141
Corner Myrtle and Lafayette   142
Rainbow   143
On Memorial Day   145
Deferred Poems   147
After the Storm   149
On a Foggy Day   151
Fall. . .   152
A Perception of Human Nothingness   153
One Day   154
Lunchtime in the Capitol City   156
Too Busy   157
To the Readers   158
A Visitor   159
Grandfather   160
At Sixty Six   161
To Aaron   162
Rainstorm   163
The Dove   165
To My Children 167
My Grandfather's View. . .   169
Waiting   170
Death   171
Contrast   172
On the S.S. Rotterdam   173
Marriage   174
Lean Days. . .   175
My Yard   176
We Are Cowards   177

At Babi Yar   178
Taking Chances   179
November Winds. . .   180
A Sign of Spring   181

Journey Ahead
The World Gathering   185
On an Ancient Road   187
To Jerusalem   188
Jerusalem Sabbath   190
This Crowd Is Ours, This Place Is Mine. . .   193
The Wall   195
World Gathering Last Night at The Wall   197
Elie Wiesel Speaks   199
After the World Gathering   201
Hebron Bus Stop   204
Mea Shearim   205
At the Foot of Mount Gilboa   207
Sinai Dreams. . . .   208
On the Golan Heights. . .   210
On the Other Side of Sambatyon   212
Second Class Citizens?   213
From Warsaw to Masada   214
Coexistence   215
Rav Turai Karl   217
The Sabbath after Auschwitz. . .   218
Tisha B'Av in Jerusalem   220
Kibbutz Gonen   221
Safed   223
Facing Kunetra   225
From Hell to Hope   226
Shehecheyanu   227

Brachale   229

Foreword

There are many ways to bear witness: One can show pictures of events; a statement can be made to the media through a news release; a proclamation can be read; and then, of course, one can document other misfortunes by writing these in one's own blood.

But in poetry, one can testify through the use of a power that is both mysterious and forceful.

Herman Taube's poems are, indeed, creative transcriptions. His words demand remembrance as they call out to a sinful and unconcerned world that would just as soon forget the events which these poems commemorate.

I am not a poet and I feel, therefore, it would be inappropriate for me to analyze or interpret Taube's free verse. For this task we have professional critics and teachers.

I can only react to his bearing witness in a form and manner that bears the Jewish seal — our people's soul.

Herman Taube's poems are immersed in Jewish suffering, his eyes search in heavenly dreams for sources of hope. He transcribes a past that has disappeared; a unique Jewish world of beauty and splendor. He portrays the sad mood as well as the spirit of hope of survivors. He strolls with his readers over the cemeteries of Europe and then takes them to Jerusalem where everything breathes eternity.

Taube's terse poems speak of a person who lost everything. We are shown the feelings and emotions of a Jew who comes back to his home town to pay respect to his lost relatives, and cannot even find their grave.

Episodes, memories, images of Majdanek, the dusty torn suitcases — the Jewish treasures in Birkenau. From Shabbat songs of decades past, he takes us to the lamentations of the present day anguish of a generation wanting to forget. Taube narrates his impressions vividly, his encounters with friends, children, unknown passersby. And does it with both sensitivity and great perception.

You imagine him as cantor standing before a congregation praying, singing about a vanished world. And despite all temptations and stumbling blocks, he writes with hope for the future.

His vision roams over many continents, countless diverse subjects, and a variety of characters.

Everywhere he finds a word, an expression, a sound, a thought, a proper noun, and together they start singing and form a poem. These poems are a witness that belong to the never-to-be-forgotten witness literature of our time.

— *Elie Wiesel*

JOURNEY BACK

Poland

"The sun rising over Poland and Lithuania will no longer
find a Jew sitting by a light in the window saying Psalms,
or at dawn on his way to Synagogue."
Yitzhak Katzenelson: Songs of the Slaughtered
Jewish People

"-Po Lin. Here will you rest,"
were God's solemn words
to my forefathers.
In this Polish countryside,
from the Baltic to the Bug River,
on fertile potato fields,
on wheat lands around the Vistula,
among farms smelling of thyme
and cow manure, we built
villages, gardens, houses of prayer,
shops for tailors and cobblers.
All we needed for body and soul
was around us in our small world.
Springtime, on Lag b'Omer,
we marched on hikes, up mountains,
into forests, listening to echoes,
voices from the wilderness,
coming back accompanied by
bird songs and the whistle of the wind.

Now, after decades away,
we have come back to visit
the countryside. Nothing has changed.
The same horse-and-buggies,
millwheels grinding wheat,
barefoot children keeping
watch over herds of sheep.
Same road, same village.
Same shops, same markets.
We talk in whispers:
where are my people
who lived here for
hundreds of years?

3

No echo. No voices.
Just emptiness inside me.
Everything is hollow.
The soul is gone from
the Polish Shtetle—
the old cobblestone streets
are sad. So am I.

On the road to Radom, Poland 1975

Evacuation

Goodbye, Cherniachow.
The Clubhouse burns,
Messerschmidts are
bombing all approaches
to the town, all roads.
The Zhitomir bridge
is on fire. People run,
abandon their homes.
The radio blasts threatening
news: the enemy has bombed Kiev.
The militia evacuates
the elderly, women, children.
Men are ordered to report
to the Military Commandantura.
I am turned away: "You are
a foreigner, leave immediately,
rush to the station!"
I look back at Cherniachow,
a peaceful town, in flames;
I mumble through tears:
Goodbye Lubimygorod!. . .

I run, following the crowd
of bieziences — refugees,
my skimpy belongings
I carry on my back in a
ripped old burlap bag.
The burnt-out bridge
lies in the river swamp.
I make a detour to a
narrow, unpaved path,
to the rail-station: Gorbashi.
A train is slowly moving,
destination unknown,
women, old men, children
huddled together in open
cattle wagons, platforms.

An old man stretches out his arm,
I grab his hand and jump
on the moving refugee train.
We pass charred wagons, houses.
It's getting dark, cool,
We hear bombs bursting,
the roar of planes, machine-guns,
our train stops in a field,
no one sleeps, no one talks.
Total darkness, utter silence.

Evacuation - II

At dawn the train moves again.
We pass charred telegraph poles,
trees, farm stables scorched
by fire, still smoking, animals,
tree roots overturned upward.
A duel erupts between planes
and guards on the roofs of our train.
We hear explosions, children crying.
The train comes to a sudden stop.
A command: All jump!
Machine-gun fire mixes with
bomb-shell blasts around us.
An enemy plane bursts in flames
and crashes. "All clear!"
We are back in our wagon.
Thank Heaven—"Chwala Bogu"—
all accounted for. The train moves.
I help the people with "first aid,"
bloody knees, arms, foreheads.
My Red-Cross armband, my medic shirt,
improves trust, friendship;
after all, I was a stranger among them,
a man of military age, going
in the opposite direction,
away from the front lines. . . .
Suspicion softens, I am accepted
as one of them: A refugee. . . .

Our train passes Kiev. No stop.
People share water, food, tobacco.
Again we hear anti-aircraft guns,
this time from a far distance.
Where are we going to? Nobody knows.
I feel embarrassed, the only young man
in a wagon of women, children, old people.
The heat in the wagon is unbearable.
I'm comforting the children, the elderly,

7

sponge their faces with cold water,
an air of sadness prevails in the wagon.
Someone starts to sing, people join in:
"When my friend will return home. . . ."
"Kogda towarish moy domoy wierniotsa. . . ."
We stop at a railroad crossing:
A military train is leaving for Kiev.
The soldiers give us canned goods, bread,
dried fish and fresh water - kipiatok.
We ask them, where are we going?
"Trust us, we will save you," say the
soldiers. "We will win this war
and you will return to your homes."
Huddled in a corner in our wagon.
I cried all night and prayed
for the soldiers going to fight
my war, my enemy. . . .God protect them!

    June, 1941

Cherniachow

The journey back to Cherniachow
was like coming back from a grave.
My short-cropped hairs were gray,
my legs supported by a cane.
Three years have passed since I left
this town: war, hospitals, pain.
My numb, swollen feet can hardly move.
As I step down from the freight train,
a silent snow greets me: Welcome back!
The locomotive says goodbye and leaves
with cars squeaking rhythmically;
the noise awakens the stillness of Gorbashi.
In my army rags I look like a scarecrow;
I follow a throng of people to the road, where
a wooden sign says "Stancia Gorbashi,
Six Kilometers to Cherniachow."
A farmer stops his buggy. "Hey comrade,
crawl on." His strong arm pulls me up.
"Where are you from, tovarish?"
"From Poland, from the war."
"Where are you going now?"
"To the Policlinic in Cherniachow."
"You look hungry." Not waiting for
an answer he hands me a sweet beet.
I can hardly understand his language,
but his friendly smile, his eyes talk.
I say: spasibo, diakuyu, dziekuje.
He smiles, there is so much pleasure,
hope and simple human goodness in
his face. "Nasha strana - our land -
suffered much, our town is racked by grief,
but Cherniachow will recover.
We'll make it together. . . ."
Stumbling in the snow, leaning on my cane,
I am almost running to the Policlinic,
anticipating familiar faces. . . .
Not one doctor, medic, nurse survived;

only the guard came back from the war.
He looks at me for a moment, grins,
grabs me in his arms, covers my face
with kisses and starts to cry:
"I lost my wife and children, my mother, brothers.
I'm so glad you survived, to see you again. . . ."
I am walking alone the streets of the town.
The parikmacherskaja-barber shop is open,
but Zienia Bolshaja isn't there any more.
I keep imagining that any moment she will
appear, tall, beautiful, always smiling:
"Come, have a haircut, for refugees half price!"
I have a lump in my throat: Where are you Zienia?

Never Again Will I Blame God

All during the War I had doubts:
Is God really in control here?
Is it He who decides the outcome of
battles, is He the source of reward
and punishment? Yes, I blamed Him.

Almost at the end of the War,
In March, Nineteen forty-five,
I realized how wrong I was:
My medical unit arrived in Plathe,
a destroyed town in Pomerania.

Enemy shells had shattered the houses,
people were struck down while
trying to escape into shelters;
they were hastily buried in pits
civilians, soldiers, women, children.

My unit gathered their remains
from the trash-pits, and those
scattered on the side roads.
At the railroad station in Plathe
we gave them all a decent burial.

In one mass grave we buried
civilians and soldiers, victims
and victors, Russians, Poles, Germans,
under one banner, saying: Remember!
For Your and Our Freedom!

Here I realized what equality means,
Here I perceived how stupid war is,
What fragile creatures we all are.
Here I took an oath: Never Again
will I blame God for the lunacy of men!

A Soldier and A Dog

This is an encounter of man with a dog:
A nameless medic and a shabby mongrel.
With tear-filled eyes he faced the city,
he had seen five years earlier, full of life,
bursting with people, trees and parks.
Now he stared at a capital—a pile of
rubbish, struck by an erupting volcano,
a war-ruined place after an earthquake.
Embraced in pain he walked the streets;
not a tree, not a moan,
not a sound, a city of the dead
the stench of burned flesh
rising into the air.

At the cemetery he noticed something moving;
she came toward him from behind wild bushes,
a shabby, hungry-looking mongrel.
She came from nowhere, stepping out of a grave,
dog-trotting up to him, smelling his army boots.
The tall and gloomy-looking man was thinking
of diseases dogs usually carry: lice, infections,
rabies-madness and flies. He was ready to
brush off the animal by pretending to
pick up a stone. But the dog's eyes
were begging food and he gave her his ration
he carried in his Red Cross travel bag.
She swallowed the morsels in an eager dash,
followed him around the huge burial place
and back to the railroad station.

The rail guard tried to scare her away
with his rifle butt, with stones and curses.
The dog kept coming back, stayed there
wagging her tail until the train left.

The nameless medic went back to the war,
thinking of his homeless, hungry friend.

When decades later he returned to the
rebuilt city, restored parks filled with people,
he remembered the mongrel who had appeared
from the conclave of ruined tombstones,
licking his boots, while he was crying
at the graves of his lost family.

Warsaw, Poland
October 1975

Vodka

On Memorial Day I decided
to clean our garage, cluttered
with mouldy, unread manuscripts,
waiting for years to be discarded.
I smelled dust and noticed a bottle
of leftover vodka. I paused.
My throat keeps burning from the dust
and the smoke on the busy road.
The dryness gnaws at my tongue,
blows dust between my teeth.
Our ambulance roams slowly, following
tank formations, torpedo cannons.
Every time I step on a stone,
roadside excavation, obstacle,
I see fire lightning before my eyes;
I get dizzy-drunk with fear, pain.
The wagon smells of blood, urine
and disinfectants that make
my lips shrivel and crack.
A cloud of smoke hangs over us,
we can't see the moon, the stars,
we move like fugitives in the night,
curled up to each other,
calming our thirst by sipping vodka.
On the thoroughfare leading to
Brest-Litovsk we hit a mine.
Our ambulance flies like a tossed toy,
spins across the road, breaks up,
and rests silently in the dust. . . .
What will not leave me is the taste of dust,
        blood and vodka.
What happened to our noble nurse, the driver,
the doctor and the patient.
I can hear them singing,
cursing, laughing and crying.
I can feel the sweet smell of vodka
we sipped in silence, at starlight,

while the bombs kept dropping, bursting.
The moans of wounded soldiers
will not let go.
The squandered years of war,
of our shattered lives, left us
flashbacks of pain, blood and vodka.

Memorial Day 1983

Last Hour in Majdanek

A sound reverberates in my ears,
an echo of a discordant trumpet
and a groan of alarming drums.
I heard them on a January morning
Nineteen Hundred Forty-Five.

I recall red-white banners, an eagle
and soldiers taking their vows
to defend their country, fight for
the homeland "until victory."

I uttered the oath, knowing
that my homeland was saved, but
my home, my family was destroyed.

I heard about Treblinka, Chelmno,
Sobibor, Belziec and Oswiecim.
Only there I was part of it, in it;
my Army base was in Majdanek.

Everywhere I went I smelled gas, the
odor of the "Disinfections Kammer,"
the smell of the barrels of human fat
destined for soap factories in Danzig,
wheelbarrows loaded with human bones,
mountains of shoes, eye glasses, luggage
destined for the "Fatherland."

I felt a mouthful of bitterness at
the open doors of the crematoria ovens.
I searched for air and ran to the yard.

There stood a gallows. A thought:
what relative of mine swayed
on this gallows? For what sin?

I stumbled upon charred limbs, on
a heap of burnt bodies, soleless shoes,
ripped caps, bloody, torn shirts.
Everything was sprinkled with gray ashes.

I didn't feel fear, hate, pity or pain,
just a frozen numbness of mind and body,
raindrops rand down my face.
My Army boots stepped on dead shells,
parts of skulls, scattered ties, scarfs.

Every piece of discarded shred had
an owner; I could see their faces, I could
hear their voices; they were my people.

The cold rain clung to my army coat -
cooled my face and made my body shiver.
But my eyes burned like hot tar, my
throat wound bled. I still kept walking.

The trumpet sounded again: Last Call!
Destination: Poznian, Berlin.
My feet marched in formation. It signified
I was still alive.

We boarded heavy Army trucks.
Soldiers sang. My throat continued bleeding.

We left Majdanek on the Lublin road.
I swallowed my own blood with the
salted taste of tears and raindrops.

Everytime I hear drums or trumpets
Majdanek comes to haunt me.
Faces of men, women, children

17

march to the beat of the drums.
With fists lifted to heaven: Why?
Asking mankind: Do not forget us!

June 19, 1983
Fathers' Day

Monuments

The Polish White Eagle, engraved in black marble
on gravestones of soldiers killed in World War Two,
greets us in Jastrowie, Blotnica, Walcz and Ploty.

With the Red Cross on our arms, we marched this region
in nineteen hundred forty-five, fought like heroes
from Pila to Szczecin, Lawiczka, Koszalin, Kolobrzeg.

We helped the wounded, buried the fallen under banners:
"For Your and Our Freedom." We buried the flesh
and carried with us their spirit: Hope of Liberation.

The tears in moments of death, hope turned into dust,
last words—Mamo, Jezuniu, Long Live Free Poland!—
still reverberate in my memory, three decades later.

Their tears turned into crystal rock, made monuments
out of grief, cold as ice, still as death, they live
entombed in my heart like a catacomb, a personal shrine.

For the young soldiers killed in the battle of Podgaje,
bound with wire and burned alive by the enemy,
my chest feels desolate like the monuments we passed.

Warsaw

To Sam Mozes

A liberated ghost town,
skeletons of destroyed buildings,
burned churches, synagogues,
shifting clouds in the grey sky
hovered over abandoned streets,
her people gone into exile.
The face of my lonely guide
expressed shock, sickness, hunger.
My lips were sealed, just tears
mixed with the falling rain.
I felt a shattering sense of grief
standing at the entrance to
the historic Gensia Cemetery.
Suddenly, I remembered Jeremiah:
"—I beheld the earth,
And lo, it was waste and void;
And the heavens, and they had no light. . . ."
I stopped at Ohel Peretz, whispered:
"Yisgadal V'yiskadash" and stopped.
I felt ignored by my Heavenly Judge:
"Because I have called and ye refused,
I have stretched out my hand
and no man attended. . . ."
I ran from the ruins in tears,
wrath and anger filled my soul,
the shadows of Warsaw's martyrs
followed me to the rail-station,
I cursed the day within my heart.

The groans and weeping
of Warsaw's children follow me
all the years of my life.

May 1945

20

Warsaw

Images are coming to greet you.
Mordecai Anilewicz and his friends
are waiting for you on Zamenhofa,
at the monument in Ghetto Square,
ready to embrace relatives who come
to pay respect to five centuries
of Jewish existence in Warsaw.

Buried beneath your feet in this ground,
in mass graves, bunkers, sewers, are
ashes and bones of a martyred people
who rose to fight their enemy
on Passover, Nineteen Forty-Three.
At the monument of bronze and granite
Malachi Anilewicz will read us
his plea to the Polish 'Armia-Krajowa':
"Give us guns to fight the Nazis.
We'd rather die in battle than surrender!"

"You Jews are drowning, we can't swim,"
was the response of the Polish command.
We will retain this reply in our memory,
carry it from the Ghetto Walls to our brethren,
a message to our people everywhere:
do not depend on nations who build us
monuments after we perish;
to hold on, help each other fight, endure. . . .

October 1975

21

The Stone

"There are stones like souls"
—*Rabbi Nachman*

On Zamenhofa Street,
Muranow district,
Warsaw, Poland,
on the site where
the resistance
of Jews against the Nazis started, April
nineteenth, nineteen
forty-three, stands
a monument "To the
Heroes of Warsaw Ghetto."
There on a cold day,
October, nineteen
seventy-five, I did
an incredible thing:
I picked up a stone—
smooth, cool, gray —
carried it with me
to Krakow, Brezinka,
Bucharest, Jerusalem,
without a visa, permit
or declaration
I brought it home.
I keep it in our
china closet, with my
Sabbath Kiddush cup,
candlesticks, and
Havdalah holder.
Often, when the house
is asleep and visions
burn my mind
I take the stone

into my hands;
like friends, we share
our secret memories.
The stone has a heart.
Inside it vibrates
a battery and a tape
which plays repeatedly
Remember! Remember!
Four hundred thousand
martyrs of Warsaw Ghetto!
Sometimes, past midnight,
I think I hear the stone cry:
Why? Why? Why?. . . .
I take the stone,
hold it to my face
and wash it with my tears.

Suitcases . . .

The Auschwitz Museum experts constructed
a pyramidal composition of valises,
travelbags with names of people
from many countries, nationalities.
It is obvious: This is done to shake
our senses, awaken our memories,
by looking at this symmetrical mountain
of suitcases under this glass display case.

I remember a brown suitcase, same size,
same shape as the one in the showcase,
sitting on the bottom shelf in a book cabinet
in my grandparents' home, in Lodz;
whenever I wanted to play with it,
I was politely dissuaded by my Zeyde:
"Zeydeshi, are you planning to travel somewhere?"
"Oh, yes, my child, very, very soon. . . ."

"The Messiah is due now any moment, any day;
we will all return to Eretz Yisroel. . . ."
I used to sit there and dream about voyages,
trains, ships, oceans leading us to the Holy Land;
for decades I carried this dream, until now;
I can't keep my eyes on my Zeyde's suitcase,
my vision is dim, fades away with my dream.
God! What happened to my grandfather's promise?

Auschwitz-Birkenau, October 1975

Avremel the Tailor

Everybody in Konstantin
knew Avremel the tailor,
"Die Sheyne Sarah," his wife,
and Friedele and Rochelle,
his twin daughters.
Their home was quite old
but well kept and clean.
Sarah was as goodhearted
as she was beautiful,
she worked from day break
until late at night, cleaning,
helping her husband, cooking
and serving free meals
to poor yeshiva students.
In her believing heart
there was one hope and prayer:
G-d would fulfill her goal,
Avremel and she would live
to see Friedele and Rochelle
under the canopy. . .
One day the whole family
was snatched away by the Nazis.
They were stacked in box cars
with all Konstantin Jews
and shipped off to Birkenau.
They ate mouldy bread and soup
made from weeds.
First Sarah got dysentery
and was taken "to the clinic."
Friedele and Rochelle
were selected for experiments
in the twin observation center
of Obersturmfuhrer Dr. Mengele.
Avremel worked in a "commando"
sewing burlap bags for clothes
being shipped to the Reich.
One day he recognized a dress

he himself had made for his Sarah.
He stopped working for a moment
wiping his tears from his face.
The SS sentry-whip came down
on his shaved head. Avremel
collapsed, blood running down his face.
"This is my Sarah's dress!" he mumbled.
A kapo began swinging with his
rubber stick at Avremel's face.
He fell to the ground and died
holding Sarah's dress in his arms. . .
The other inmates were jealous:
"Er iz geshtorben wie a Mentsh!"
He died like a real Mentsh!. . .

Yankel Wassertreger

He carried this heavy pail of water
From the well in the market place
To the homes of the rich in the shtetl.
He knew what was cooking in every pot,
Who was getting married, who was "with child"
And G-d forbid — who will die. . .
He established a waterprice scale:
For the rich — a groszen for a bucket,
For the poor: two buckets for a groszen,
For the Rabbi, the widows and elderly
He delivered water without charge,
Claiming: "He up there is paying. . . ."
When people asked: "Why Reb Yankel,
A man like you who knows how
To read the holy books, decided
To become a wassertreger?"
He answered in humility: "A man
Is doing what it is destined for him,
I serve my G-d and my community."
He died while hurrying water
To the synagogue, where the Bet Midrash
Caught fire. In his little shack
They found a pail full of groszens,
Attached to it was a note addressed to the Rabbi:
"I collected the groszens
Not for the water but for carrying it
To people's homes. Please use the money
To help the widows, the elderly and
The poor among us."

Ozorkow 1945

A Single Hair

"No crown is simpler
than a single hair."

Wallace Stevens.

Sir, Excuse me.
You, Sir.
With the camera on your shoulder.
You are a tourist, aren't you?
Here! Please, look here!
I know it's hard for you to see me. . . .
You're looking at
the full window display of HAIR
in this museum.
But this is me. . . .
Please look closely, see
a hair sticks to the glass,
almost off the frame?
I know it's hard for you to see me
with your naked eye.
Me, among a mountain of hair. . . .
Especially when all of us look
so frighteningly the same:
ash gray.
Actually, we all were
of different shapes and colors:
blond, brown, red, black.
The "Zyklon B" gas discolored us all.

For eighteen years I lived
on a girl's scalp
among braided hair,
pitch black, like yours,
matter of fact.
This is why I have decided
to talk to you . . . .
People come here daily,
like to a zoo.
Take pictures, eat ice cream,

28

listen to guides, tapes.
They never, but never, notice me. . . .
For thirty-two years now
I have stuck to the glass
with the hope
that someone will pay attention
to Me, an individual hair.
After all,
I had a life of my own.
You know, Sir,
I was such a silky,
soft, glossy hair.
Often combed by a mother's tender hands,
caressed by the boyfriend of the girl
whose head I adorned.
Even so, I was only one stand of many thousands.
He found me among her braids,
played with me,
affectionately rolling me
on his finger.
Together we had so many dreams,
hopes, visions, aspirations. . . .
The girl whose head I adorned,
her mother, the man who loved us
and I
were all taken to this place.
We were sorted, separated
by selections.
Maybe you will see parts of us
in the other displays:
ashes for the fertilizer show window.
The glass case of soap
called "R.I.F."
I survived, managed to stay out of a hair mattress
I was selected for. . . .

Oh, how much I'd like to get on the outside,
be warmed by the sun.
I dream of wind, thunder.
This glass display will crack,
break into pieces. . . .

The wind will pick us up,
carry us, scatter us,
to all corners of the globe,
disperse, hair by hair,
to all capitals,
blow us into the eyes
of the world's leaders. . . .
Just to irritate them, disturb their vision
enough, to make them feel
a little sting, burn, hurt. . . .
Draw a few tears
out of them
for me,
for all the millions of hairs
blond, red, brown, black,
who turned ash-gray
because of "Zyklon B" gas. . . .
You know? No one cried for me
with real tears. . . .

Sir, I see a glossy look
in your eyes.
I hope You can spare one for
me. . . .
Sorry if I did upset you.
It is so lonely here,
among this mountain of hair. . . .
I wanted so much to live,
to grow, to form new hair
on an eighteen-years-young
girl's scalp. . . .
Forgive me for being personal, Sir.
Have you someone dear
who has long hair?
Please, when you see her,
touch her,
think of me, remember me,
a little hair
in the corner
of a showcase
in Auschwitz. . . .

Rabbi Moses Isserles O'H

Crakow 1520 — May 1, 1572

A facade of tombstone walls
leads to the cemetery grounds
where you are buried.
A small synagogue built by
your wealthy father in 1553
still stands here, some relics
survive, chandeliers, holy books,
a reminder of past lifetimes
when you studied here, molded
Jewish Law for generations to come.
From here philosophers, kings,
scientists gained recognition,
immortality for your "Holy Community
On the Vistula and Volga Rivers."

A granite monument marks the place
Where your heirs, Jews of Crakow
in groups of ten — a minyan —
were brought here during Nazi days
for daily executions in this court.
Today, a group of American Jews
came to pay homage to You —
the great historic codifier,
and the small number of lonely
Jews from nearby towns who returned
from the partisans, concentration camps,
to find nothing but your tombstone. . .

Maczej Jakubowicz, an Auschwitz survivor
greets us in the shul court:
"We are fragments of old melodies
the Remo sang here centuries ago.
We will not disappear from our
people's memory, we cherish our past
and look to the future with hope
even when the present is dim. . .

31

This tombstone of Rabbi Isserles
has a message to you: ZECHOR
Do not forget the past!"

Rabbi Yehudah Ajzenberg Z"L

August 22, 1942 dawned humid and hot,
a mass of exhausted three thousand
Jews of Lask were marched to Chelmno.

They were ringed with somber looking
guards armed with rifles, whips, dogs,
and SS commandos carrying machine guns.

Aching women were holding on to the
tailclothes of their men and half-naked,
thirsty, hungry children followed them.

The townspeople watched through windows,
hardfaced neighbors silently waved goodby
to the Jews on their WEG Zur EWIGKEIT. . .

Among the people walked the rabbi of Lask,
the renown scholar Reb Yehudah Ajzenberg,
a name famous in every town in Poland.

A Polish guard offered the rabbi a seat
on his horse-driven wagon, among the old,
sick and the people unable to walk.

The rabbi declined: "I rather walk with my
people, they need my prayers, my presence."
He knew where his people are "resettled to."

At an abandoned farm they called a rest,
the rabbi noticed the camouflaged guns,
hidden on the trucks surrounding his people.

He realized that his kinsmen are doomed.
Reb Yehudah asked the guard for permission
to pray. The guard responded: "Make it short."

The rabbi raised his hands heavenwards,
swaying from left to right, intoning a nigun
— a melody from the morning prayers:

"They are taking us to the Chelmno Camp," —
the short, slightly built rabbi was shaking:
"But not all of us must perish in this churban."

"I beg you kinderlech, run, hasten to the woods,
take your chance, have no fear, we are three
thousand, they are only thirty executioners."

"Yes, they will kill some of you, but run, jump,
leap to the forest, G-d be with you, run!"
The young began to run, the rabbi continued:

"My dear fellow Jews, we have nothing to lose."
The surprised guards opened fire, frightened,
shrieking with rage, they let loose the dogs.

Of those who escaped that night, some survived
to recount the story about their beloved rabbi
Yehudah-Leib Ajzenberg — of blessed memory.

On A Journey Back Home

To Abraham Goldkind

The window of my home
faced a small park.
My grandmother used to
sit there and enjoy the
panorama of tall trees,
young women with babies,
old men resting on benches,
white pigeons, black crows
chasing each other in groups.
On Saturdays and holidays
the small park was jammed,
people would stroll calmly,
laughter, songs filled the air.
The happy voices reached up
to my grandmother's window.
She would sing with them:
"Wos geven wet mer nit zain —
"What was, will never be again. . . ."

I returned there decades later,
the tall trees are gone,
no people, no more benches,
just an empty piece of ground.
I was told that the Nazis
made the people dig deep pits,
buried them all in the park.
The following spring the trees
would not bloom, they died.
The birds did not come back.
They cut down the tall oaks
and erected a monument to
the martyrs who are buried there.
Passersby seldom stop there,
children are afraid to play;
They say that at night you
can hear children's voices crying.

Henoch. . .

To Henoch Wigodsky

"No one kneads us again out of earth and clay, no one
breathes into our dust."

Paul Celan: "Psalm"

Beneath closed eyelids
I see my friend Henoch
dressed in white shroud,
trembling from fatigue,
his forehead still bleeding.
He is waiting to be called
by Cherubim and Seraphim
to the Heavenly Tribunal.

For four decades now, his soul
wanders between hell and paradise
waiting for admission. . .
The world is denying Henoch
ever existed, Heaven has no room
for a humble student.
There is nothing sacred about him,
no piety, no good deeds are registered
in the records of "The Eternal Kingdom"
to make him eligible for paradise
to rest among the "righteous . . . "

He was a student of Torah
ready to become a teacher
when the war erupted in 1939.
He was not doing any fighting
or helping his community,
but running from Lodz, Poland
on Tuesday, September 5,
he was hit by a German salvo
in Brzezin, on the Warsaw road,
and buried in a mass grave
among many unidentified refugees
in the Lodz cemetery.

36

I remember Henoch's handsome face,
He sang songs of love and lust,
He had great dreams, ambitions, hopes.
Now, decades are fleeting by.
Henoch is not allowed to pass
the many eyes of the Angel of Death
whose guards of cruel, dreadful demons
hover between heaven and earth
with their swords drawn. . .
Henoch's life is not remembered
by any one but me, his friend.
His family perished in Majdanek. . .

Oftentimes, I see him in the clouded skies,
or when I awake in despair at midnight.
Beneath my closed eyelids, Henoch appears,
dressed in white shroud,
his forehead still bleeding,
He clings to the doorknob of Heaven asking
for a little space for his soul. . .
But angels Uriel, Raguel, Raphael, Gabriel
are overloaded with similar lawsuits
before the Heavenly Tribunal.

Sunday, April 22, 1979

37

My Girlfriend

"My love, my love, why have you left me alone?"
James Joyce

My girlfriend, loyal schoolmate,
I remember your loving face
in the moonlight, your tears,
gentle kiss and warm embrace
the night I went off to war,
taking with me your smile,
your promise of eternal love,
leaving you my solemn oath
to return someday, in peace,
to be united forever!. . .
A blitzkrieg defeated our Army,
divided, disgraced my country,
I was wounded, but survived
and after years in combat
I came back searching for you.
They told me you had been taken
from Ghetto Lodz to Majdanek,
or Chelmno, or Auschwitz. . .
I returned to my army unit
stationed at Majdanek, Lublin,
a former concentration camp.
I saw mountains of shoes,
crematoria, gas-chambers
disguised as "Disinfection-Kammer II."
I was ordered to shower there
with my fellow soldiers,
inhaling the fumes of "Zyklon-B" gas
still shrouding the undressing room.
Entering the shower chamber
I imagined that you were with me.
My lungs burst, I suffocated.
Sonderkommandos take my corpse,
separate our entangled bodies with axes,
they cut my fingers, to remove
the brass-ring you gave me

38

the night I promised you eternal love.
My body is removed
to a chamber for my hair to be shorn,
my corpse to be buried in a pit.
In the flames our souls were united.

Auschwitz-Birkenau, January 1945
translated: November 11, 1979

Way Home

I sneaked up the stairs,
like a thief, to the top flat,
scared I would collapse
from shortness of breath, tension.
Finally, I saw the familiar green spot
on the brown door-frame,
the space where the mezuzah was mounted
by my grandfather decades ago.
On the door was a note:
"Mommy, I went to church to choir rehearsal."
The longing and the dreams
which pulled me here across continents
were reduced to nothingness. . . .

My trembling fingers touched
the green spot on the doorpost.
Hastily I ran down the curved stairs,
pursued by shadows, images
of my former neighbors.
In anxiety I stumbled and fell,
cried for help from growing pain.
No one was there. The little girl
in my grandfather's flat
went to church, to choir rehearsal. . . .

Decades later, I still dream about
a brown door-frame with a green spot
where my grandfather's mezuzah used to be.
Often, when dreams carry me way home,
when I see my family, neighbors,
I'm unable to control my tears of anger.
Yet I still have the habit of touching
with my fingertips the mezuzah on doorposts. . . .

Zawadzka 29,

For decades I had this hidden desire
to visit my hometown, Lodz.
A pipeline to my subconscious mind
kept alive the imagery of an
obliterated past; a house at
Zawadzka Twenty-Nine.
When finally my dream was fulfilled
a cold shiver ran down my spine,
I lost all confidence in my strength
when I approached the building
where a chunk of my childhood lay.
Filled with consternation, emotions,
a heavy heart and tears took over;
Here was my grandfather's apartment,
the Prayer House, the Kindergarten,
all in one, tall building.
I wanted to be alone, and told my guide
to leave. He looked at me amazed;
A grown man so timid, ashamed of his tears.
I stood there overwhelmed by memories,
I remembered Wacek, my next-door friend,
his hair was white as mine was black.
Wacek and I had our own hiding place
in the fifth floor attic.
He owned pigeons and a pair of rabbits
and he let me feed them.
We shared his fruits and my challa-cake.
A spark from the past came to me;
Pani Zosia, Wacek's mother; tall, blond,
strong and beautiful, came up to the attic
with a basket full of laundry
and found me in a corner crying.
It was a week after my mother died. . .
She took me in her arms, talked softly;
"Nine-year old boys should not cry,
this was the Lord's will, your mother is now
united with your father in heaven . . . ."

41

I don't recall any more all the other
words Pani Zosia said to me that morning,
I do remember her warm tears
falling on my face. . . .

The Messiah Came to Europe

The Messiah came to Europe,
according to tradition,
ready to redeem humanity,
declare everlasting peace.
He wandered the streets of villages,
looking for his people.
Mystified, puzzled, hurt, he called:
Father Most High! Your children
are nowhere to be found!
I came to proclaim, according to Thy will,
the Kingdom of Heaven, Resurrection
of Your loyal servants. No one
reawakened from dusty ashes
spread as fertilizer on European fields.

At the gates of the European cemetery
He found a survivor, who asked in anguish:
Why didn't you come when needed?
Up to the doorsteps of the gas chambers
our people sang "Ani Ma'a min — We Believe."
Sadly the Messiah listened to the lonely
survivor, tears running down his white beard.
I have no answer to your crucial question;
I myself must repent and ask their forgiveness.
Until then, my redemption be suspended!

Washington, August 29, 1978

43

The Chosen People

"O God of Mercy, for the time being Choose another people. We are tired of death, tired of corpses, We have no more prayers. For the time being choose another people."

Kadia Molodowsky

In my miniature work and reading room,
hangs a picture of my grandparents:
Zeyde Reb Gershon-Leib, and Bube Mirele —
Olehem Hasholom — of Blessed Memory. . . .

Grandfather's snow-white beard and eyebrows
look at me with the sadness of the day
I had to leave home, four decades ago.
He must have known I would never return.

Every time I stare at his gentle features,
my emotions are overtaken by grief,
my calm is troubled, my mood disturbed:
something in this picture is irrational. . . .

My esteemed grandfather worked six days a week,
observed Shabbat, Kashrut, gave charity,
was called: Talmud Chacham — Talmudic Scholar,
Lamdan — intellectual with a capacity to teach.

My grandparents liked to help people in need;
there were always 'orchim' — guests for Shabbat.
My zeyde was one of the first Jews of Lodz Ghetto
chosen to be destroyed in Chelmno Concentration Camp. . . .

The Struma

Hearts are growing uneasy
facing The Struma Monument.
It's hard to calm aroused,
stirred emotions when reading
seven hundred sixty-seven names
of children, women and men
engraved on this tombstone.
The names cry out their protest,
tell the story of the Struma:
A disastrous voyage of Jews
escaping from Constanza,
after brutal persecutions.
People slaughtered, synagogues
razed, homes looted, Jews hanging
from meat-hooks in windows
of Bucharest butcher shops
bearing signs: "Kosher Meat".
The Struma Monument talks of
British cruel insensitivity
to the suffocating refugees,
who, after two months suffering
on the overcrowded boat
Struma, were torpedoed
outside the Istambul harbor.

The Turks accused the Germans,
The Rumanians blamed the British,
Had we Israel at that time
the Struma people would have been saved.

Bucharest, Rumania. October 1975

45

Numbers

A sightseeing bus rides leisurely, slowly,
on cobblestone streets in old Bucharest.
Forty pairs of eyes have their retinas set
on side street panoramas: ancient dwellings,
people. They deposit snapshots in their minds,
images, imitations of life in Eastern Europe,
memorabilia to take back home to the States!

In the rear of the bus three men converse
in subdued voices, negotiate numbers.
They speak of "Israel's unfavorable balance,"
"numbers of housing units needed for absorption,"
and of "social welfare, training, learning,
challenge, fulfillment, future" and: numbers —
the price we must pay for being Jewish!

"I came with you on this purposeful mission.
This shows you how much I really care," says
the man in the middle to the others.
"Yet, I have my own style of Jewishness.
I just had four hundred guests at my daughter's
Bas Mitzvah, you should have heard her speech."

The bus stops at the Joint Distribution Center;
forty pairs of ears listen to greetings, eyes watch
aged, lonely people, remnants of Rumanian Jewry,
sitting quietly on benches, waiting for their numbers
to be called. In a dignified manner
they will choose an array of attire,
household needs, pay for it with free coupons!

A number is called, a woman gets up;
she is tall, slim, her face delicate, pale
her hair neatly combed, eyes brown, sad.
We notice a number, bullet marks on her arm.
Politely one inquires: May we ask who you are?
She understands English, but is reluctant to talk:
"I have reasons for not wanting to give my name."

"My family was well known all over this country,
my father was the. . .No! I better not say.
I am the only survivor of a town nearby.
I need a warm garment, the flesh wounds hurt.
My town's store always runs out of sweaters,
when it comes to my number, my line. . . .
I asked the JOINT for help. Here I am!"

"But you're still young, why live alone?"
"Sir, I was seventeen when this number was branded. . . .
I was selected for another mark on my breast. . . .
When I resisted, they opened fire. . . .I survived,
was taken 'for experiments' by Dr. Joseph Mengele. . . .
Nothing is left in me to share. . . .You see, dear man,
this is the price we paid for being Jewish!"

Bucharest, October 1975

A Lonely Bird

> "In a swamp in secluded recesses,
> A shy and hidden bird is warbling a song."
> *Walt Whitman*

On a windy October day, on a lonely tree,
in the yard of the Nozik synagogue in Warsaw,
a black bird was shivering on a naked branch.

"Haven't you seen the cold days coming?
Why didn't you join your flock," I asked,
"when they flew off to warmer parts?"

"Here my nest was safe, lined with grass and leaves;
nearby is a garbage pile with plenty of crumbs
to last for a lifetime. The trouble is

I forgot about the wind, snow and winter,
I didn't think of the cats and dogs around here,
who hate lonely birds.

Now it is too late to leave, the feathers on my wings
are too old, too weak to fly against the wind.
Say, have you any crumbs you would like to share?"

Warsaw, October 1975

DARKEST LIGHT

Letter to a Poet

To Chaim Grade

Shall you ask:
How long will we continue
to bemoan our past?
Your question answers
itself: Forever!
I will write endlessly.
Pain, strife, ugliness
of war and hate,
cannot be written
by historians alone.
We are the witnesses.
Like you, I'm pulled apart
by opposing
desires; I strive for love,
happiness to share with
my wife, children, friends,
or sit and write about
the despair of our people.
I am a self-imposed
codifier of chaos,
so preoccupied with pain
that I condemned myself
to solitary exile.
My poems are my enemy;
they rob my precious days
left at the gate of life.
Writing about the past
defies all logic, sense,
I'm in a spider web,
entangled in images
who haunt me, hold me,
calling, demanding:
Write! You are our memory!. . .

Together

Together we stand, shoulder to shoulder,
building new life in the land of the free;
our hair is gray but our voices still strong,
when in unison we sing: "Oh say, can you see."

We are a unique mass of survivors, people
of different shapes like the stars above;
yet we are one united family when we sing:
"G-d bless America, land that we love."

Our memory is made of steel and iron crust,
we don't forget and don't forgive the tyrant;
we likewise remember our liberators — the just,
when proudly we sing: "This land is our land."

Our blood is still rebellious, seething with
memories of times gone by, years of hurt and pain;
now, together with 'The Generation After' we
    march singing:
"O beautiful for spacious skies, for amber waves of grain."

Rockville, Maryland. October 1984

52

Silence

Today I watched two women meet —
last time they had seen each other
was in a concentration camp: Stutthof.
They hugged, laughed, shared memories,
looked at old pictures of lost friends.
Then, they stared at each other and
there was no sound — a deafening silence.
The blackout of words lasted an eternity,
a noiseless dialogue between past and
present; the invisible victims and survivors.
All I could hear was a subdued teeth-crunching
and the quiet, resigned dumbness of tears. . .

American Gathering of Holocaust Survivors

Hilda Thieberger

"To Erwin, with love. . ."

You're two minutes in her home
and Hilda is already dancing
around you with a platter of
food, cookies, drinks.
You set foot on her doorstep,
touch her cheek with a friendly
kiss, and you feel at home at once.
Sit with Hilda five minutes,
and you're back four decades,
in fourteen concentration camps.
She is like the pelican
who, according to legend,
tears open its breast
to feed the young with its
own blood in times of hunger. . . .
Hilda broke all Nazi rules,
walked over forbidden borders
to find food to sustain her child.
Her home is full of pictures
of her children, grandchildren
and the art work of her husband.
She loves the present, but,
always thinks of the past. . .
the agonies of her tormented
family, ravaged by the Nazis.
There is an abundance of love,
striking humbleness in Hilda.
Like her Erwin, she carries
no grudge, no hatred for anyone.
There is grandeur in her smile
after so many merciless years. . . .
The constant looking back to
the extinct past, combined with
the will to live and love is
the secret of Hilda's survival.

December 28, 1979

Contradiction

F. N.

The words "surrender" and "endure"
are equally embedded in her life.
Her emotions lack conciseness:
Sometimes she is extremely soft,
occasionally hard like a rock.
Her imaginary feelings sound real
and her life is dominated by nightmares.
She tries to suppress the pain
with an extreme willpower to live,
always searching for a shimmer of light
in the dark clouds of memories.
To capitulate or outlast
her past and present: She cannot live
with one without the other. . .

She never attended a synagogue service,
never fasted on the Day of Atonement,
Sabbath for her is just another day.
She does not observe any commandments,
disregards persistently any prayers.
But on Yom Hashoah — Holocaust Memorial
Day — she lights a yartzeit candle.
Her nights are full of horror dreams,
childhood experiences prey on her mind.
In the morning she dresses fashionably,
teaches French in a local college,
and looks genteel, refined and soft-spoken.
She volunteers her free time to speak
at school assemblies about the Holocaust.

In her poetry she releases innermost
emotions: Loneliness, fear, and betrayal;
she is the victim, the witness, and judge.
The Auschwitz furnaces, the Majdanek ovens
were destroyed four decades ago, but

in her heart the flames are smoldering.
She is a mature, enlightened woman,
only when alone, she is a child still
taken by force from her parents.
She cries inwardly with anger:
God! What did You do to my mother?. . . .
I am a grown person and I miss her,
I cannot forget her, I need her so much. . . .

The Only Jew in Town

"A people that shall dwell alone and shall not be reckoned among nations" (Num. 23:9)

He came back from the war,
his family, his friends were dead.
He chose to live, reconstruct life.
The people around him were sick,
thin, gaunt, with haunted looks
in their eyes, constantly hungry.
Having served as a war-medic,
he opened a shelter for the homeless,
a first-aid clinic and free kitchen.
The refugees kept coming, crept in,
stretched on the bare benches.
From sunup to sundown, he worked
feeding the hungry, helping the ill,
preparing the food, cleaning the shelter.
Batch after batch of poor vagrants
kept coming, shivering from cold.
In spite of pains from his war-wounds
he continued compassionately his work.
He felt no bitterness or hatred toward anyone.
They too have suffered in this war.
Still he was a stranger to the local people,
wasn't welcome in their world.
He felt like a man in a pit looking up
at a mountain top he can't reach.
Their gaze was ice-cold, motionless
like rock, deathly stiff.
Every morning, when he opened the door
to the clinic and shelter, he implored:
"G-d! Change my facial expressions
from fear to trust, cover the shadows
of sadness, remove grief from my brows
to conceal the past torments of war. . . ."
Did Heaven listen to his prayers?
He began to change, to smile again.
He helped to rebuild the town, the clinic.

Times changed, but not his neighbors. . . .
They walked by with ice faces, not a nod
of greeting to the only Jew among them. . . .
Their silence became frightening, hazardous.
He realized he wasn't welcome.
He left his town forever!. . .

Plathe, Pomerania, 1945
translated: November 1979

Encounter with a Rocking Chair

I rested for a moment in the study
of my children's home, in a rocking chair
that belonged to my son-in-law's father.
I closed my eyes and journeyed back
half-a-century, when the tick-tock
of my grandfather's clock was part of me
like the squeak of the rocking chair.

My grandmother was listening to the
whisper-prayer of "Va'yeten Le'cha"
on Sabbath night. She was humming the
melody of "Gut Woch" to the chair's motion.
I never knew what stimulated her,
the swaying of my grandfather at "Havdalah,"
or the chair itself — gift from her mother!. . .

I remember her rocking as if she were in
convulsion, brokenhearted, when my mother died.
The chair squeaked loudly, as if crying,
expressing her feelings. She sat there
quietly, lips locked up, eyes closed,
only a tear sitting on her cheek.
The chair did the lamenting and sighing. . . .

I know what happened to my grandparents
but I don't know what happened to the chair.
Was it used to heat a room in the cold
winter nights? Or, did a soldier
ship the chair to his wife in Germany
as an antique decoration, a war relic
from occupied Litzmannstadt?

July 20, 1979

59

March 10,

To Susi

This morning you told me
to wish you Happy Birthday.
"On March 10, 1945 I was liberated
from Stutthof Concentration Camp —
I stopped being inmate #61856
and became again my human self."
For the first time in three decades
you talked openly about the camp
not mentioning your grandma,
your mother, sister — of blessed memory.
There was no hate nor fear in your voice
when you spoke of attacking soldiers
how they raped the "fortunate" girls
who survived until the hour of liberation. . . .
Memories gone forever? No!
You carry them in your brain,
your bones still ache, your skin branded,
reminiscences like silent movies
are running constantly in your thoughts
even when you talk about grandchildren. . . .
Memories grow old, we have learned to live with them,
the pillow on your bed is salty from tears.
Many times I hear you weep in your dreams;
I don't dare awaken you, not knowing
what is more real: your crying in the night,
or your voice singing in the morning.
Today you went to the hair-dresser,
to visit friends and our grandchildren.
I went to services to bless the day
of your liberation and to say Kaddish
for all those who did not live to see
March 10. . . .

A Survivor's Husband

To Susi

Often at night,
I hear you sigh,
it sounds like weeping,
groaning. You shriek out
brief sentences:
Riga, Kaiserwald,
a ship named "Bremenhaffen,"
a camp named "Stutthof."
You yammer about
a raging war, cities crumbling,
mothers raped, smothered babies,
men, women driven
into the Baltic Ocean. . .
I wake up when you scream,
look at your beautiful face,
listening to your heavy breathing,
I curse and hate your dreams
who torture you
for decades now.

Morning after
you dress in style,
your eyes glow,
laughing, hurrying to work,
you deal gently
with your customers,
charm them with your smile.
But I carry all day
your fears and grief.
Your memories, like heavy rocks
pull me downward,
torment my soul,
patiently I bear the load
of your pain,

I pray every day
for peaceful nights;
for the past
to pass away!. . .

Visiting a Home in Sao Paulo

To G. H.

I visited a lavishly furnished home,
surrounded by palm trees, tropical flowers.
I caught a glimpse of the paintings,
art and sculptures by the great masters
and was impressed by the rare manuscripts
on the massive, brazilwood book shelves.
We sat on an elegant leather sofa
looking at albums of decades ago;
pictures of your relatives; you knew
nothing of how they died in the Holocaust.
Between the reading of letters
from your brother, your murdered mother,
in the midst of tears and memories
we shared, your maid appeared, announcing,
"Dinner is served, kindly join us!"
While walking to the table, I wondered
if the Nazis, after killing our mothers,
also went to their dinner tables
as calm and composed as we did?

After dinner we entered your library:
The mahogany bookcase reached the ceiling;
the crimson rug outlined the features
of a Slavic monarch, with mustache
and eyebrows turned upward, his drawn sword
ready to strike at anyone disrupting
the muted stillness of this room.
We sat on your velvet sofa and read
the titles of your books,
inhaled the odor of ancient volumes,
dealing with war, blood, Holocaust.
You spoke quietly, shared memories
of the Nuremberg Trials where you
were a witness for the prosecution.
I watched your face while you were reading:
so much beauty and pain,

63

tension, grief mixed with subtle charm.
I appreciated the pleasure of seeing your
original Chagall's, Picasso's, Katz's,
Van Gogh paintings, sculptures,
the artful lamps and Indian carpets.
Yet, from every corner of this home
shadows of the past stared at me:
Poland 1939. Auschwitz-Birkenau 1944. . . .

I was frightened by the monarch on your rug,
the crimson spots looked like chunks
of human flesh, like spurting blood of your
mother's bleeding wounds, when she was taken
from Block Eight to Auschwitz' crematoria.
The passing decades, distant continents,
the camp-number on your arm, since removed,
could not dislodge your dear mother's imprint
    on your mind.

    Sao Paulo, Brazil
    November 10, 1980

Letter to a Survivor

To Eugenia H.

You're walking a tightrope
over an abyss of memories,
trying not to lose the balance
between the ugly past days
and the blessing of renewed life.
You still walk "through the valley
of the shadow" of the camps,
remembering dear ones who perished,
while enjoying your family and home.
In a world so fragile, full of sorrow,
your past is magnifying its imperfections,
plugging daggers into your pulsating heart;
recollections that make you bitter,
moody, guilty: Why did you survive?
It hurts to see your home, fit for happiness
with the man of the house sad and sick,
It aches to see you, a gentle, perfect lady,
with scars on your arms. . . .
Your antique, mahogany book shelves
are full of volumes about SS monsters,
their ghosts hover over your expensive bed.
Your mother comes here every night, incognito,
past the security man guarding your home.

Sao Paulo, Brazil
November 10, 1980

65

On Vacation

I am plagued by fearful
visions of the past,
they meddle with my present.
Everything I touch,
every desire, idea, dream
I imagine, want to believe in,
lapses in retrospect.
I look at ordinary things:
a flashing sun, and think
of crematoria heat.
At night, outstretched
on a folding chair
in my back yard,
the moon floating, it seems,
in the darkness, I am reminded
of torture chambers,
solitary confinement.
I try to read Shakespeare,
but Hamlet looks pale
when Babi Yar, Birkenau,
keep hovering inside my head.
This morning I tried Kafka.
I like the way he writes,
for an instant I'm transformed
into the hero of "The Castle."
Still, my senses are unmoved,
frozen, paralyzed, by bygone days.
Even Tolstoy's *War and Peace*
looks bloodless.

August 18, 1978
Rockville, Maryland

California Condors

We are an extinct, scarce tribe,
like the California Condor, few
of us are left in this world.
No one cares about our survival,
some would prefer if we vanish.

The darkness of our eyes haunts
and makes them feel uncomfortable:
We know too much about the past.
Some species call us vultures,
they admire us when we are in flight.

Some are scared by our presence,
when we dive and nest in their field.
They're frightened when we hunt
for creatures — our enemies who made
our kind an extinct breed. . . .

Encounter with a Friend

In memory of W. W.

I was eager to visit my friend
I hadn't seen for half a century.
He survived the war, married rich,
they live in a beautiful mansion.
But, I felt cold and strange in
his home: everything is so artificial,
decorative like his wife's make-up.
My youth-friend is exalted by sports,
attracted to guns, rifles, swords;
the walls of his club-room are full
of certificates, prizes, plaques,
a display of trophy cups for winning
sharp-shooting competitions, mounted
mementos of animal-hunting games. . . .
We both were soldiers in the war,
where our friendship originated.
Yet we come from different upbringings:
he looks down on men who cannot fight.
"The world despises people who are weak,"
he says with a dark light in his eyes.
He speaks of judo, karate, fencing.
I feel so strange on his soft chair,
deeply embarrassed by my ignorance
and the paintings of bloody bullfights.
I remember that in my old home
the place of honor was reserved for
books: the Bible, the Talmud, classics.
The only picture that adorned the wall
of my grandparents' dining room was
a portrait of a rabbi teaching children.
His bearded face follows me like a vision
now, after a distance of six decades.
I realize the power and influence of
my grandfather's books and the picture
that dominated the wall in my home.
In the classroom where I teach,

68

I feel his presence, his spirit.
My friend will remain my war comrade,
but our ways are worlds apart. . . .

My friend died from heart failure
while duck hunting in N. Virginia.
His widow offered me some of his plaques:
"I'm selling the house and moving
to Florida. Who needs all this stuff?. . . ."

Insects Won the Battle

"God is the mystery of life, enkindling inert matter with
inner drive and purpose."

Rabbi Mordecai Kaplan

Our tormentors called us vermin,
identified us as disposable matter,
germs, insects to be exterminated.
We coped with wind and winter,
the darkness of the Holocaust.
We survived the inferno like snow-flies,
like ladybug beetles beneath the snow.
We outlasted our enemies, resembling
tiger-beetles in larva tunnels deep
underground, wrapped in rags like
moth-pupas wrapped in leaf cocoons,
weathering the storm hanging on trees.
Our bodies were skinny like the praying-mantis
persevering inside the hardening egg cases
on stalks. . . . We outlived the human beasts
as goldenrod gall-flies survive
in a larva inside hollow ball-galls
in goldenrod plants. Our lives
were hanging on thin, silken hair,
like cabbage-butterfly pupas, attached
to weed stalks by silken slings.
We persisted. The insects won the battle:
Our tormentors perished, We Are Here!. . .

Self Portrait

Posture: twenty pounds overweight.
Face: an open book, sad but friendly,
retouched by color reservoirs of past,
framed with multigroup of pictures,
my wife, children, grandchildren, friends.

Voice: emotional, screeches tantrum-like
when angry, likes to give vent, dispose of stress,
smashing frustration, inner hostility, with words.
But not as frightful as I sound, my children
still like me singing lullabies, Sabbath songs.

My accent sounds like cracked porcelain,
expensive, precious crystals, yet damaged,
false notes in a choir and orchestra, singing
opera arias slapstick style. People smile politely;
I feel inadequate, guilty, emotionally hurt.

Attitudes: thoughts, values — old European
literature, religion, customs, life styles
left their fingerprints on my soul — mother's
Yiddish songs, grandfather's melodies — Zmiroth,
still share my celebrations, happy moments.

Mind: no rubber-stamp or carbon copy,
always like to take advice, listen, learn.
The more I learn, the more I like to know.
My actions are triggered by my beliefs,
and I believe in people, friendship, love.

Character: dislike ethnic jokes, making fun
of others harbors prejudice, hostility, hate.
I'd rather be silent than tell "popular" stories,
I had my belly-full of insults in years past
to last for my lifetime of sad remembrance.

My eyes enjoy looking at facial expressions,
they are fascinated by the sight of birds, trees.
Often I close my eyes and daydream, see visions:
bridges built in the air, people holding hands,
all races, colors, holding on, helping each other.

My ego does not seek status or recognition.
I respect others for what they are and do;
I never knock other people, pulling them down.
Yet I don't like to be ignored or belittled.
I am kind, modest, just do not humiliate me.

This is my self portrait in black and white.
Still, there is another likeness hidden in me;
a picture of a whole family who perished in war,
from hunger, hate, fear, and only I survived. . . .
This family photograph torments my mind.

My smile will never be full.
In my eyes there will always be gleams of sadness,
at every merry occasion,
for the innerworld of my forefathers, still
living, continues to the end.

I Am a Poet

To Arnost Lustig

I am a poet, a microcosm of my own,
my brain gives birth to ideas,
my tongue brings forth words,
my eyes see visions, images,
discover stars, planets of the sky.

With my pencil I create and destroy,
invent and terminate love and hate.
In my world I make Pythagoras
and Aristotle sound wrong:
Heaven is no higher animal to me.

There is no right and left,
right or wrong, front or rear,
top or bottom, face and back,
length and breadth to the heavens,
there is only what I want to see.

I decide how many stars there are
between the equator and the Antarctic Pole.
Only the plants I see exist,
only the trees I plant grow,
only the people I create are real.

I take from nature
only what I can absorb. The rest
of the stars, sun, earth, I leave
to other microcosms. The sound of streams
is for all to share.

The Centerpiece

To Susi

Among the paintings in my home,
crystal, silver cups, art objects,
hangs a picture I call the centerpiece of my life.
While working at my desk, typing,
reading, writing, talking on the phone,
wherever I move my body
the gleam of her beautiful eyes
guides me like light. . . .
I'm forever thankful to my friend
Pedro Lopez, who painted this portrait for me.
When I feel lonely,
her face cheers me up.
When I write poems or stories,
my instinct draws inspiration from
her likeness. It represents affection,
and elicits my admiration for that woman:
Her humility, the delight on her face
make me love her dearly, deeply.
Sometimes I get bowed down, depressed,
I feel a need for encouragement,
all I do is look at my centerpiece
and I feel energy flowing to my heart. . . .
How fortunate I am to possess this portrait,
how lucky I am to have the girl in
this painting as my companion for life.

January 9, 1982

Sadness Looks from Your Face

To Arnost Lustig

From the bottom of my heart,
where all my poetic notes float,
from my mind's secret hiding place,
where all my thoughts rest,
I am moulding a poem just for you.
With my pen and paper in hand
images, echoes turn into words,
senses take on form, lines,
like an artist drawing on canvas.
You are in a good tempered high spirit,
warm, cheerful, your face pale as
your white hair — you laugh,
pretend cheerfulness, but
after five minutes your eyebrows
change position, like the drama
mask in a theatre: Sadness looks
from your face.
The look in your eyes speaks
louder than your lips.
The cheerfulness is an act of
cover up. The signal from
your eyes beams with their sad lustre
a message stronger than the loudness of
your good-humored voice.
Oh, how would I like to leap
over that gate — that facade of your face —
cut out all the bullshit,
put my arms around
your shoulders and ask you openly:
Friend, what hurts beneath the chin
of this good humored face?
But you have your own secret hiding place.
Your mouth is open, your words
eloquent, your jokes good humored,
but your thoughts, a hidden pain —
a certain tension — mysteriously

is omitted from our conversation.
I feel so inferior for not being
able to gain your confidence,
your friendship, strong enough
for you to share the source
of the sadness in your eyes.

Abraham Sutzkever

Creator of compositions:
mystical, romantic, poems
so simple and appealing.
You are always searching,
striving for certainty,
attempting to find new
tones, new words in old
styles, forms of the past.
Your troubled, soul, the
sadness of the Holocaust
comes through your poems.
Not only are the writings
exemplary, but your life,
your actions: The dedication
to the memory of our people,
lives in your creations:
Survival, Resistance, Love,
the rediscovery of our past
continuation of "the Golden
Chain" gives us a sense of
supernatural beauty, soul,
faith in Netzach Yisroel.
While others are preoccupied
with physical survival,
you carry the torch of
remembering our culture
with talent, hope and joy.
You keep Yiddish alive
as a sacred language of
a people of sacred martyrs
and heroes we must never
forget. Precisely, therefore,
we bless the hour when
you, Abraham Sutzkever,
survived, to guide us. . . .

You returned, a biblical Ezra,
wanderer from thorny diasporas,
echo of burning ghettos, ruins,
a disinherited son came back
to claim his legacy, Yiddish.

You resurrected Peretz's "Golden Chain"
with weighty poems, inventive rhymes,
a reservoir of talents, ideas,
a blend of thoughts, courage, faith,
a source and sight of bright hope.

From feathers you revived a bird
who sings to us forgotten melodies,
every stanza, story, new essay —
a prerequisite to Mama-Loshon's
redemption and perpetuity

Janusz Korchak

Guards standing all around
pushing people toward barbed wire:
Deportation Point-Umschlagplatz.
Crowds carry their possessions:
prayer-shawls, phylacteries, books.
The "haupt-artz" Nahum Remba,
pushes his saintly figure toward
a children's formation marching
with fear on their innocent faces
toward cattle trains.
"Where are they taking us?" — some ask.
It seems awkward to be going on
a picnic in such filthy, smelly wagons.
But they don't panic; their teacher
and guardian Janusz Korchak walks along.
Weary is his brow, despair, grief
is written on his face, but
soft and calm his voice. . . .
Remba grabs Korchak's arm, whispers:
"Look dear Janusz, don't try to
be a saint. You know where
these tracks are leading. There is
no way you can help your orphans.
We want to take you out of here
so you can write, survive this war."
"My dear Remba, useless are your words.
If my children are in a grip of death,
I will not deceive them, or leave them.
I doubt if I could carry the burden
of living without these little hands.
No force can keep me away from them,
their fate is my destiny. . . ."
Children climb into cattle cars, some stumble, cry,
they are pushed into the wagons by the guards.
Janusz Korchak follows them, the cars are shut,
in the darkness dry mouths complain; no air,
little hearts beat with horror, weep loudly.

In the midst of the blackness, a familiar voice
asks them to sing the new melody they have learned.
Voices of boys and girls spread over the platz,
the throngs of people are listening in silence,

the SS-henchmen, gendarmes can't believe their ears.
All turn their faces to the moving cattle cars,
youthful voices penetrate the air:
"ANI MA'A MIN. . .I Believe. . .ANI MA'A MIN!". . .

Your Junk Man

He is tall and thin,
his face adorned
by a wild, gray beard;
thick eyebrows cover
his sad bluish eyes.
Dressed in rags
he follows the
horse-driven cart
through side streets,
back alleys,
calling with his
hoarse, deep voice:
"Junk man!
I buy, sell everything!"
Five days a week
he trades his trash.
Friday noon he
sells his "stock"
to the junk dealer,
turns in the rented
horse and cart.

Home, he takes a bath,
combs his beard,
changes his clothes
into a Sabbath garment,
locks himself in
his spiritual domain
with his Bible.
He reads aloud
the chapter of the week
with a melody
he learned in his youth.
His day of rest,
like his Bible
and prayer shawl,
are not for sale.
Sabbath he is King.

Images

I

Images hound me,
tarry my dreams,
disturb, distress, choke
me, like batches of snakes
creep all over my mind,
scold me for sins
never committed,
longings never fulfilled,
love never consumed.

Images of friends neglected,
teachers disrespected,
neighbors evaded,
a friend in need,
disregarded, abandoned,
a visit, a phone call
postponed. . . .Their images
come at night,
at quiet moments,
disturb my conscience,
torture my heart
with guilt, blame, fault.

Images of fingers,
pointing sharp lances,
daggering my dreams,
grasping, holding me
from dusk to dawn,
cleansing my soul,
while tormenting me
with Images, asking:
Why? Why? Why?

II

With clicking sound
strikes the clock,
with rhythmic beat
like my pulse.
A likeness
framed in black
leaves a mounting,
starts to float
in pitch darkness,
hovers in my room.

Eyes flicker, sparkle
with a gleam,
lips tight, face gloomy
like the blackness
of the night.
Illusion clear, real:
A likeness floating
on a stream,
two hands extended
beg, try to reach me.
I can hear a scream
of horror, grief, fear.

My senses awaken,
the likeness fades,
disappears.
Now the Images
settle in my mind.
Nightmare, tick-tock
of the clock,
is taken over
by the rhythmic beat
of my heart. . . .

To the Image in the Mirror

I
Image in the mirror
Fellow homo sapien
This is not an urgent plea
Not words of praise

No hymn, not a ballad
To be set to music
No cry or comment of despair
Just a warning, a prediction

In free verse, an alarm sound
For you, Image in the mirror
For your eyes and ears
To see, hear the roar

That agonizing scream
Of a man in death pangs
His sufferings drown
In a sea of silence.

"Liberty, Human aspirations,
Right to free expression"
Are void, hollow sounds
Greeted with neglect

By the world's mighty
From the Vatican Palace
To the skyscraper called U.N.
Are YOU among THEM?

II

Fellow human species
Who hide in caves
Called split levels,
Ranchers, colonials

Cuddled like hermits
In high-fenced yards
To camouflage your
Tennis courts, pools

And close your auricle
To protect yourself
From the weeping, calls for help
Afraid that a molecule

Of human kindness
Will penetrate, uninvited
Into the chambers
of your cerebrum.

To you, who turned
Your backs on fellow humans
Insulted, tyrannized
For wanting to live free

Or the right to leave
To you, Images, likenesses
In the mirror, my warning,
My premonition

III
Your offspring will breed
Image, blank, dry eyed
They will thrive on
Frigidity, characters cold

As the marble
On your sink tops
Your kin will be
Dumb, deaf and voiceless

Mouth, lips, tongue
Will move, gab, rant
And no sound will be heard
They will inhale smoke

Of your neighbor's house
And not feel the smell
Or heat of fire
All they will see

Is their own Image
in the silver-lined mirror
All they will hear
Is the splash of their

Own bodies in your pool
Your own kind will
Call, shriek for help!
Drowning, Falling, hurting

IV
You will not hear his cry.
For too long, You
Framed their mind
To turn your back

Pretending nothing happens
nothing can befall You. . . .
Then, you will start to scream
Your lips will move

No sound will come out
Only deadness, muteness
As you were silent
To the cry of your

Fellow homo sapiens
When they were craving,
Begging, calling for help
There will be no one

To answer your call
Your Image silenced forever
Shall turn into shadow
Of nothingness.

The cave
Your palace and your mirror
Will remain,
without your Image. . . .

Two Stones

To Henry Taylor
/dialogue/

Minute by minute they live: The stone's in the midst of al.
William Butler Yeats

I

I am a stone stiffened
by millennia of
ravaging hurricanes,
earthquakes and
unpredictable changes
in the universe.
You can find my kind
on the moon, stars, earth,
hard as a rock,
not afflicted by age,
dominant in the world's
development, progress.
Historic epochs, mountains,
parks are named after me,
I helped build pyramids,
temples, palaces,
from time immemorial
to this day.
I was used in war
to destroy and kill,
in peace to construct,
fashion and beautify
interiors and exteriors
of dwellings, shacks, mansions.
My desire is now
to be used in a fireplace
where I will feel
warm in winter,
cool in summer,
will listen to good music,
see love-making,
hear songs and human chatter
by which my stony heart
will be warmed.

II

My origin is as solid
and stonelike as yours.
My genesis goes back
to the Eolithic periods.
I was used for gravestones
for Abraham, Jesus, Mohammed.
Mosques, churches, synagogues
were built with my help.
Still, I'd like to continue
living on the road,
kicked by human feet,
run over by tires.
I'd rather be free,
warmed by the sun,
or feel the snow,
be washed by the rain,
see the moon, stars,
and hear every morning
the birds sing. . . .
Fame, origin, make no sense
if all you retain
is a corner on a fireplace.
I'd rather live in danger,
fear, see the changing of seasons,
lie low on the ground
and be able to look
to the heavens above.
And think that on all
revolving stars
there are stones.

A Fourteenth Street Personage

They call him: "Whitey Wino."
He is a distinctive figure
on "K" and Fourteenth.

He walks slowly, carries his
belongings in a shopping bag.

His disheveled clothes show
bare parts of his unwashed body;
pedestrians step aside for this tall,
thin and odorful personage.

While people rush to work, to stores,
offices, hotels, and cafeterias,
Whitey Wino inspects garbage containers,
looks for food, discarded beer cans.

Merciful hearts cry out with sympathy
for the victim of society,
disposable like the cans he collects,
crazy, peculiar Whitey Wino.

John Smith, alias Whitey Wino,
strolls on Fourteenth Street,
looks at "Soul Brother" epitaphs
written on walls of abandoned buildings,
stores ravaged by anarchy in years past.

Women hang around bars like flies
around dung. They walk the pavements,
approach cars, offer their femininity
for a price, under the watchful eyes
of pimps and drug pushers, while
plainclothes police are following their actions.

John Smith's heart cries out with sympathy
for this regimented society,
crazy, peculiar world.

Holes in a Pot

Some of us are
like holes in a pot,
sitting on a stove.
The burner holds us
on a palm of fire.
We can smell the food
burning, smoking,
feel the heat —
turning a meal into steam,
the cookery running out,
boiling over, escaping. . . .
We'd like to stop it.
But we are nothing,
just holes in a pot
sitting on a stove.

Yoachimowicz

I

People treat him with affection,
he captures their heart with his
poems, short stories, common language.
Long after the full auditorium's applause,
his lectures, verses, readings
linger in their minds like melodies. . .
But like a lonely cat, he lives in
a kind of solitary self-confinement,
with no allegiance to anyone.
He sits on his back porch,
ignores the phone, fan letters,
he lets his recollections travel
to bygone times, when his poems
were living, loving people
and not dimmed echoes of the past. . .
His memories, erased by time,
are like recharged batteries
generating determination to live,
to choose, to write, to speak.

II

My friend, a genuine Yiddish poet
lapsed in obscurity, keeps on writing
calamitous, rigid stanzas about
the obliteration of Yiddish culture.

He is obsessed by the destruction
of the shtetls and laments our loss;
His poems are not troubled by lack
of talent, but the erosion of readers.

I asked him: "Why pursue writing
if there are no more Yiddish readers?"
"If I can't write what hurts me, why live?
My poems are my own survival!"

Who Am I?

A man of piety complained to the Baalshem, saying: "I have laboured hard and long in the service of the Lord, and yet I have received no improvement. I am still an ordinary and ignorant person."
The Baalshem answered: "You have gained the realization that you are ordinary and ignorant, and this in itself is a worthy accomplishment."

Hasidic Story

— my longing for compassion comes
from my grandfather — olov hasholom.
He loved humanity, was always ready to help;
a peaceful, cheerful man, never angry.
I remember him when my mother died;
he tried in vain to calm my grandmother
in his low, soft voice, his gray eyes
glossy with tears. It's G-d's will!. . .

— my roots spring from the subsoil
of a cheder-school and yeshiva pews;
chassidic rabbis spread mysticism in my soul;
the subtlety of my teacher's learnings,
the ipcho-mistavro contradictions,
philosophical disputes follow me
like a guiding light all my years,
influencing my ideas, opinions, ideals.

— my learning of Jewish history by Dubnow,
the writings of Peretz, Ash, Dinenzon, Bialik,
keep flowing in my soul like a refreshing stream.
I remember many of their stories, characters,
Broderzon's rhymes; odes still revolve like
a spinning record in my mind. My mother's lullaby
was the melodies of the cantors Kusevitski,
Yosele Rosenblatt; I still love to hear their records.

— my interests now lie in helping others;
I enjoy sharing with your mother "nachas gossip,"
the satisfaction we get from your letters,
or sharing with you news about our family.

When time permits, I read Chaim Grade, Sutzkever.
The Bible still inspires my fancy, uplifts my spirit.
I would like to write a good book about the past,
I doubt if I can do it; yet, I dream about it.

from a letter to my daughter Miriam. . .

To Judy

There are men who suffer terrible distress and are unable
to tell what they feel in their hearts, and they go their way
and suffer and suffer. But if they meet one with a laughing
face, he can revive them with his joy. And to revive a man
is no slight thing.

Hasidic Story

There are many attributes of piety;
you can express emotional ecstasy
by loud singing, by intense swaying.
"Set all the limbs of your body astir,"
and speak to Him in any tongue.
Yet, the wishes and prayers He accepts
and responds to are the language of love!. . .

You can find thought and communion
with Him in a soft, silent devotion.
Don't extol Him to the skies, looking
for the Almighty on a Heavenly Throne,
His presence is everywhere.
You can feel and see it right now;
time and space vanish in His presence!. . .

Just turn your eyes to the person
next to you, shake his or her hand,
catch a glimpse of your neighbor's
face, smile and say: "Good Yom Tov!". . .
Hold the person's hand, sense a vibration,
This is His spirit, His goodness,
the splendor of the Creator lives in you!. . .

Look into the mirror of your friend's eyes,
and you will see God's creation: your image.
Say inwardly, with sincerity, silently:
"I love you". . .This is all that our faith is;
"V'ahavta Lerayecha Kamocha —
love your neighbor like yourself,"
Love your people, the world, and you love Him!. . .

Maryland University-Hillel
Elul, 1979

Confidence

"Man is born to free choice, to believe, to doubt, or to deny. I choose to believe."
  I. B. Singer

Every morning I watch the sun
rise on the horizon; a red ball
coming up slowly on a blue firmament.
Sometimes, gray clouds overcast
the daystar, fog dims the view,
yet, I know the sun is there,
her rise unchangeable, irreversible
like my belief in the Almighty,
Who now and then hides His Light
from me, makes me stumble in darkness. . .
Still, I know full well He is here;
I am able to get up and walk.
Like the sun, His Countenance
will shine again for me. . . .

Spring

Who said that creation
ceased on the sixth day?
Come, look out my window:
You'll see Him continuing
His unending task: Flowers,
trees, coming back to life.
Rain, wind, thunder, lightning,
stars shine through clouds.
And in early morning, birds
build nests, singing, whistling;
everything comes alive,
from a blade of grass to
a larva on a tree.
That I am able to smell
and hear and feel the
fresh air and write down
what I see, all this is
a manifestation that His
Countenance is everywhere.
I feel exuberant faith
and sing inwardly: Hallel!. . .

Zechariah Came to Brooklyn. . .

— and a voice was heard
in the Jehoshafat Valley;
Zechariah son of Jehoiada,
arise from your tomb, go
to a place called Boro Park,
repeat to the zealot vandals;
"Why transgress ye the
commandments of the Lord."
Why do you smear swastikas
on Houses of Worship?
Tear up holy books
and insult pious sages?
Zechariah came to Brooklyn,
chastised the untamed clique
who spread hate, falsehoods
perniciousness to their own people.
— and as in the days of the
Temple, the zealot fanatics
"conspired against him
and stoned him with stones."
Again Zechariah's blood
began to seethe, and the
flow of tears did not cease.
Pious sages came to cleanse him
before taking his body
back to his eternal rest,
but every time water
touched his forehead,
the crusted blood reddened again
The sages pleaded;
Zechariah Ben Jehoiada,
for millennia our people
were oppressed, abused,
tombstones overturned,
synagogues ravaged,
why can't you rest now?
Zechariah responded;

"Here *Jews* are cursing *Jews*,
Rabbis are assaulted
in the name of our Torah. . .
therefore I can't be appeased."
Zechariah's soul still hovers
over Boro Park, Brooklyn.
His voice, an echo from the past,
is calling in despair,
"Breeders of brotherly hate,
who eclipsed your eyesight
with so much malodorous venom?"

I Am a Dandelion

Through times that wear and forms that fade,
Immortal youth returns.
Ralph Waldo Emerson

Alone, I am a dandelion,
the furry particles my deeds,
the seed balls my days.
They fly away, scattered by the wind.
My deeds become seeds
for the trees to grow, plants to bloom,
other dandelions to rise up
to mature and scatter seed.

Alone, I am a dandelion,
an interesting, beautiful, original,
fascinating, composite plant.
Actually, only a weed, fragile —
the slightest breeze and
I am blown away.
Yet as long as I hold on
to my roots, nothing can destroy me.
As long as my stem is
in the ground, I will grow again,
tomorrow, next spring, next year. . . .

Alone, I am a dandelion-
an empty center of a weed,
an image-one rain drop
can make me fall apart.
Yet, in gardens among my fellow
plants, I am strong.

The certainty of faith
is my source of hope-
a forceful energizer
to overcome a tragic past:
images of dandelions
blown away by the wind of war.

But they also believed
"with perfect faith"
that as long as we hold on
to our roots, we will
grow again, live again. . . .

LIVING SHADOWS

Tashlich

To Susi

We shiver in the rain
and cast bread crumbs
into the polluted Potomac;
we throw our sins into
the murky river and pray;
"He will subdue our iniquities:
and thou will cast all their
sins into the depths of the sea."
While we read, I try to remember
some of the sins that I'm repenting.
The Potomac minds her own business,
runs her own swollen path.
I watch others perform this ritual.
I feel terribly guilty and silly
for coming here in the rain
to confess, beg for forgiveness
for sins I can't remember. . .
Suddenly, I find my fault;
I have left my wife at home alone.
All year I have excuses —
my job, my work demands it,
but why did I leave her today?
I rush home to find a full house,
my children, my wife waiting.
I greet them all with a hearty
Gut Yom Tov. Happy New Year!
At Tashlich I realized how much
I sinned this past year
by not sharing in your loneliness. . .

105

Nei'lah

Wherever a man stand to lift his eyes to heaven, that
place is a Holy of Holies.

S. Ansky

The sun descending settling
on the roof of the synagogue.
The cantor faces the open Ark,
his exhausted voice sounds hoarse.
My lips are dry, mouth bitter,
my irritable tongue feels
a burning sensation, sends flash
signals to my brain, while my stomach
blows shofar. A realization:
what it is like to be hungry. . . .
The sanctuary doors are closed,
I feel like Jonah in the whale's belly.
A thousand people pray here
and I feel lonely, uncertain.

After a day full of prayers,
a thunderstorm of psalms, poems,
an avalanche of biblical passages,
showering my G-d with compliments,
praise, petition, lamentations,
exhausted from memorial chants,
confession of sins never committed,
I reach the last page of the Machzor.
I close my eyes, frightened by the thought
that the liturgy I have been chanting all day
is not sincere, the words not mine.
Angels, hell, paradise, seem far away.
Now, in the last moments before
the Ark is closed, I pray:
Simple words, children, people, earth,
sunshine, health, love, peace:
G-d — I say — make me wise enough
to care about others who are hungry,
good enough to share my love
with the less fortunate in this world.

The Shofar sounds "Tekiya Gedolah,"
people around me shaking hands,
wishing me A Happy New Year, Shalom.
Once more loneliness has taken leave.

Yom Kippur Eve in a Temple

In my synagogues
I don't have to pray,
or do anything except pay
for my High Holy Days seats.
Keep an appearance to
the blowing of the Shofar.
Kol Nidre and "Yizkor"
and my good year is guaranteed.
The Cantor, the choir and
our distinguished Rabbi
are doing the singing, praying,
repenting and all other
"spiritual things" our fathers
did in the old days. . .
Our Rabbi is a down-to-earth-man,
Knows that there is no enjoyment
In a service lasting six hours
and a sermon about sin,
spiritual evil and other topics
you are bored with on High Holy days.
Mind you, I am not trying
to escape the "annual appeal"
our president makes every year.
I am not an escapist with
an unreachable heart. . . .
I buy a "Bond" and
give a nice donation
in Memory of my parents —
may they rest in peace.
I inscribe their names
in a "Memorial Brochure"
or whatever it is called.
(My advertising manager
does not like the "brochure";
You can hardly detect the names. . .)
I was willing to donate
a full page with my parents'

pictures in full color. . .
I wanted to show our Rabbi
how much my parents were
dear to me.
But the Rabbi objected.
Like I said, He knows best
and nobody reads the brochure
anyway. . . .Who wants to be reminded
where he comes from?. . .
To tell the truth, I wish
I knew how to read Hebrew,
the original prayers.
The melodies bind us together. . . .
I look at the faces of
people on Yom Kippur Eve.
I ask myself: How am I
related to all those Jews. . .
I think of this moment
when in all remote corners
of the earth we, Jews,
sing the same melody. . . .
It's a mystery, isn't it?
In this moment I feel
a complete Jew.

A Visit to a Friend's Sukkah

To Phyllis and Chaim Lauer

In the car I was humming Maimonides'
Twelfth Article of Faith: "Ani Ma'a min."
The melody, originated in Ghetto Warsaw,
became a hymn for the Jews of Europe
on their way to the gas chambers.

I don't know why I have chosen
to sing "I Believe" on Hol-Hamo'ayd
on the way to a Sukkas reception.
Some inseparable triad from the past
lingers in my mind and memory.

The more significance holidays assume,
the more visions, melodies from the past
come up from the depth of my soul.
I sing long forgotten Chassidic "nigunim,"
feel the presence of relatives long gone.

We reach our friends' comfortable home,
three little girls greet us with smiles,
Dvora, Adina, Aviva, escort us to the Sukkah
full of guests drinking wine, eating fruits,
served by Phyllis with warmth and kindness.

After drinks, we talk of virtues
that have molded our lives: charity, holidays,
observances that have uplifted our spirit,
from antiquity up to our own times, we feel
good here: faith is rooted in every corner.

While my friends talk about charity
The words of Schneir Zalman return:
"The Shekhinah is revealed neither in the Torah
nor in prayer, but only in Tzedakah."
(How many decades ago did I read this?)

110

Chaim wistfully explains the meaning
of Etrog, palm, myrtle and willow branches.
He demonstrates the complexities
of how the lulav is waved, but my memory
keeps returning to Schneir Zalman:

"Charity is the soul and substance
of all mitzvot — all good deeds."
Chaim continues to explore the Sukkas Feast.
What a marvelous sight it was to see,
the Aquatennial — Simchas Beit Hasheiva.

Chaim's face shines when he speaks of
The Feast of Tabernacles in the Temple.
We listen with fascination about ancient
Jerusalem, we feel a closeness with the past,
again something in me sings "Ani Ma'a min"!

I close my eyes and can see my grandfather
surrounded by pious men singing hymns
in a fragile hut covered with pine leaves,
a small sukkah decorated with paper chains,
colorful stars, dry fruits, vegetables.

Chaim continues to explore the "species"
surrounding the lulav, comparing them with
the conception of unity of Torah, Judaism, Israel,
and again I see my Grandfather quoting Schneir Zalman:
"Charity brings light, understanding to the soul. . . ."

Listening to Chaim, I realize once more we are the
continuation of our people's traditions,
by observing, holding-on, singing about the past.
I understand why "Ani Ma'a min" re-echoes
in my mind on the night of Hol Hamoayd Sukkas!

Hol Hamoayd Sukkas 1979

Hoshana Rabba

Low clouds hung over
Zawadzka Street in Lodz,
bustling crowds rush
in orderly routine,
among them, the serene
figure of my grandfather
strolls to the shtibel —
the House of Prayer.
On his slender shoulders
weighs heavy the fringed
tallis — his prayer shawl.
Since today he is the cantor,
he wears a kittle, a white,
shroud-like robe.
His head is adorned with a
round, black velvet hat
worn on holidays by Polish Jews,
I walk by his side holding
his lulav, etrog and willow leaves.
My zeide is absorbed in thoughts
that he shares with me:
"Today is Hoshana Rabba,
last day of Tabernacles.
Today man's fate is decided:
set down in the heavenly books.
The "kvitlach" — the decree slips —
Float down to earth. . ."
The morning traffic fills
the street with noise,
roaming youth on their way to school
ridicule our dress, make fun
of my grandfather's beard
and my long earlocks.
But my zeide is detached from earthly
things: "Today" — he continues —
"If we pray fervently, with heart
and soul, we can still change

the heavenly decree and shape
our destiny for the coming year.
With our Hoshanas today we can
make the Messiah appear. . . ."

On the Other Hand

To Ida Kay Saks

— "On the one hand
we compare our beliefs
with a barrel of old wine,
watched over by our sages
to preserve its purity.
On the other hand
our young generation —
intellectuals, teachers —
cannot digest the strong flavor
and want to dilute it,
try to make it a drink
for ordinary minds.
On the other hand
our rabbis are worried
that they will water down
the wine's delicacy, taste
beyond recognition.
They demand that the barrel
not be tampered with.
On the other hand
many good people insist
that no one can claim
ownership of the wine;
let our children drink from it
as much as they can take.
On the other hand
many of our young do not
like our wine altogether;
they drink from bottles
with strange contents.
This brings us to our
one-hand Problem that
the Messiah will have to resolve.

So on the one hand
we keep arguing, debating, reasoning,
on the other hand
we gear ourselves to his coming!. . .
Bimhey'ra Beyomey'nu, soon!"

Yiddish

To Rita Rubenstein

"Poet, take the faintest Yiddish speech,
fill it with faith, make it holy again."

Jacob Glatstein

I

Intermediary among my people
in many lands,
a simple language
with more heart than reason.
Every word symbolic,
every line a song that penetrates
deep into my soul and keeps singing.
A lingua franca that interprets Torah,
Talmud and commentaries:
a manner of communication
in the market place and in travel.
One word. Oy!
Opens doors and hearts,
makes strangers, exiles,
feel like relatives redeemed.
A language for Chasidim
cabbalists, poets, dreamers,
revolutionaries, philosophers,
tailors, cobblers and musicians.
Yiddish, Voice of millions
who perished in the Holocaust,
sound of prayer and hope
which helped us survive, live!

II

I spin my fantasies in Yiddish,
a language infused in my soul.
"Mother" and "Mother Tongue," one origin,
left their imprint on my life.

116

Mother's soft voice sang in Yiddish,
overflowing with her love my youth.
When I pray, sing, create, dream,
my mother's legacy is always here.

My Zeyde's comments, my Rebbe's discourses,
Aunt Rachel's songs, Peretz's stories,
a language made holy by millions of martyrs
Are light sparks between the shadows.

Maoz Tzur

To Adele

My children, sing this old song
along with me.
I learned it as a child
running free,
a happy boy,
with a dreidel toy:
Maoz Tzur! Rock of our Salvation!

Later, a thousand miles away
at a cold Siberian bay
shaking in every bone
I sang it alone
with the same glow
of decades ago: Our
Maoz Tzur! Rock of Salvation!

Afterwards, in a hospital room
I shared with an army friend
a "landsman" from my city
dying from pain. For pity
while wheeling him to his rest
I sang to him from my past;
Maoz Tzur! Rock of Our Salvation!

So children, this old song
sing with me,
a melody that will never die.
May the words sound clear, high
from the abyss to the sky.
Young and wise, voices rise;
Maoz Tzur! Rock of Our Salvation!

Monologue by a Lonely Man...

Lonely am I,
Lonely is my life
Eternally...
H. Leivick

"Is it dishonest to pretend you believe,
just to be with people of your kind?
Look at me: I'm old, just lost my wife,
I have nowhere else to go, no children.
I was an active, lifetime socialist,
but all "ism's" were dragged out of
my soul during the Holocaust years.
I saw the dehumanization of whole nations.
I stopped depending on people...
I started to believe that there is
a Master of Eternity who keeps track
of all occurrences, that destiny
is predetermined by His rigid rule.
But, I see the faces of hungry children
on television, in newspapers. I listen
and see mob-demonstrations incited by
religious fanatics. I wonder: Is this His will?
When I hear the bigots talk in His name
I'm ready to indict Him for Genocide...
In the meantime, I come here daily
to resurrect my wife, I say Kaddish
weeping inwardly, my tongue moves imperfectly
muttering the Aramaic hymn for the dead.
My soul is torn, hurt, afraid:
What if there is Nothing? Why pretend I believe?
But, if you take this place away from me,
what is there left to live for?...
No! I must be wrong!...There must be a G-d!
I need Him so much, so much!

B'nai Israel, November 1979

119

I Feel Guilty

I feel at fault for the dull,
flat rhetoric of my English.
I use simple, everyday language
to relate visions, echoes, images,
in fragments of an absorbed
vocabulary, which are actually
a reverberation from the Yiddish.
The only reason I write in English
is to find a way to my students,
who simply don't understand Mame Loshon.
Of course, they think that my "notes"
have their own form, grandiloquence;
they take my inadequacies in English
as expressions of my unique talent.
I am sorry for them, I feel guilty.
They don't realize that they are
reading Yiddish in a very primitive,
poor, deficient translation.

What Is Torah?

A young man was asked by Rabbi Yitzhak Meir of Ger if
he had learned Torah. "Just a little," replied the youth.
"That is all anyone ever has learned of the Torah," was
the Rabbi's answer.

Hasidic Story

My learned friend Ezra Mariamow,
a new immigrant from Russia,
asked me a simple question:
What is Torah?
A book written by Moses?
Ten Commandments inscribed
on two stone tablets?

I quote Abraham J. Heschel:
"Torah is light, order, peace,
universal law, love, a power
that lifts you to heaven and
brings G-d down to earth.
Torah is food for your soul,
understanding for your faith,
warmth when you are cold,
water when you are thirsty.
Like wine, it makes you happy. . . .

Torah is a source of goodness,
changes pagans into High priests,
makes humanity and G-d
inseparable from nature.
We are free and exist only
by the virtue of Torah —
the bridge to His love.
Awe, joy, happiness, piety, friendship,
social and personal order.
It gives us endurance under torment,
guarantees us eternal survival,
unity with G-d, our people
and Jerusalem, His eternal dwelling."

121

For Ezra, my humble, unassuming friend,
the quotation was too overwhelming,
"Please," — he asked — "say it in more
simple words I can comprehend."

I cite an excerpt from Hillel:
"What is hateful to you —
do not do to your fellow,"
And Akiva: "Love thy neighbor
as thyself. . . ."
And Ezra has a smile.

Playing Games

To Vivian Rabineau

"A man possesses only what he gives away."
Elie Wiesel

We, who can differentiate good from bad,
who can distinguish darkness from light
try to find among sinners an iota of grace,
because in every human being is a spark of G-d.

Our feet are on the ground in dust and dirt.
Often they drag us into an abyss of despair,
but we are also blessed with a mind, endowed
with a heart that ascends toward heaven.

Kindness, enthusiasm is contagious and spreads.
Every time we perform a good deed redemption
        comes close,
like playing a game. We fill a square and our chance
of winning grows. We convince the Redeemer to come.

The Messiah hesitates: arrive or tarry?
He waits for us to decide that we really want him.
We must take part in this continuing game;
redemption is a process that follows action.

If we promote justice, speak up for human rights,
befriend a homeless stranger, giving him shelter,
share kindness, love with the less fortunate among us,
we take our place in the game of redemption!

A Common Man in Search of G-d

From a letter to Ben Saks

"Do you understand what I myself cannot even begin to
understand?. . ."
Elie Wiesel, A Beggar in Jerusalem

I am a saxifrage plant
growing flowers, currants,
among stones and rocks,
despite Arctic weather,
in the world around me.

I am a chunk of butter
in an overheated skillet,
melting away, like floating ice
in springtime, when rivers, sea
waves, flood the land around them.

I am a paradox, torn between
my grandfather's legacy:
humility, love for fellow man,
and mistrust of new ideologies,
idols or revolutions.

All week I wait for Friday Eve,
and Saturday synagogue service;
in the sanctuary I get restless,
bored by long sermons, rituals,
readings of ancient petitions.

Yet, while I skip prayerbook pages,
in my heart I communicate with G-d,
create my own psalms, questioning,
wondering: what is true, real?
what is exaggerated, irrational?

Occasionally I get entangled
in a web of anxiety, fear;
emotions reach a peak of tension;
my distressed soul leaves
the external, present world.

It hides in past, imaginary precepts,
a pomegranate full of contradictions,
unbearable to carry. Torn
between my reliance upon You and the
inconceivable realities I once faced:

Krystal Nights, Babi Yars, Ponars,
in all forms, shapes, pains.
Still, I accepted You, as I claimed my mother.
In my dreams angels zealously
protected me and You in me.

I was told that we are created
in Your Image, endowed with a soul,
wisdom coming from Your source.
You blessed us with imagination,
and I still dwell in darkness:

I cannot tell nor describe You,
My light, my Divine Creator,
do You speak to me through Angels?
Is the wind Your messenger?
the birds? oceans? sun? moon?

Is Satan — the Yetzer Hara in me,
the demonic force who destroys
my integrity, weakens my willpower
to pray, to learn, to serve You
creates chaos, decay in my heart?

All those thoughts, questions,
pierce my mind everytime I cover my head
with a skull-cap, when I enter a Temple;
I want to pray and my tongue freezes,
my soul rebels against Your actions:

I was told "seek good and not evil"
my beliefs were molded by hopes
that You are the Judge of Righteousness.
Nevertheless, Your human messengers
showered us with disaster, oppression.

What cardinal sins have we committed
to deserve the martyrdom of Birkenau?
What covenant did we violate
to be punished with gas chambers?
exterminated like a heap of worms?

If "All things belong to Him,
and He is the Lord of all"
were the creatures in junker boots
your emissaries, complying with Your orders?
Is this Your mercy? love? justice?

Maybe someday I will be deemed worthy
to understand Your actions.
Until that day I will go on arguing,
like a son with his father
to the Infinite — Blessed be He.

From Doubt to Faith

To Myra Sklarew

You wanted to know
what makes me tick,
what touches a chord
and stirs my blood.
— I live on a reserve
of burdensome memories
amassed in dark times.
They are the power
that excites, provokes,
and stimulates my actions.
Memories that shattered
lives of our people,
are like splintered
flower vases.
The vases are broken;
the scent hangs on . . .
The older I get —
the more I remember.
The more I remember —
the stronger I get!

Friday Sunset

On Friday I leave work early,
to be home before sunset.
I cannot describe the colors,
shadows of the firmament:
I watch the sun disappear,
crawl behind the trees on
the horizon in my yard,
taking the warm rays with her.
I feel happy for getting
through another long week,
that Shabbat rest is coming.
The sun, so far away cannot
be touched, but that fireball
seems so near, mine alone.
It hides behind my home
until dawn the next day.
I beat the sun in the morning
getting out of bed early
awakened at dawn by birds
singing, whistling, "Mode Ani."
The sight of the sun
the sound of the birds
makes me join their singing
Lefanecha Malekh Chai Ve'Kayom!

A Vision

When Angel Azrael
will be ready
to present me
with his death warrant
I will not object
to sinking into a grave
or being cremated
and returning to dust.

Before breathing my last
I will ask the angel
to leave my soul alone.
I wish my spirit to hover
over book shelves in a library
or in a House of Learning;
I don't mind the odor
of old, timeworn classics.

The moth-scented pages
of ancient volumes
written by my rabbis,
beloved writers, sages,
will be my companions.
I will converse with them
in silence, inhale their thoughts,
and go on living beyond time.

A Prayer

"Prayer, Man's Rational Prerogative."
Wordsworth

Bless us with the capacity
To remember and to forgive:
Bless us with the ability
To listen and understand

Bless us with the talent
To master the vocations
We are fit for and still
Attain humility of soul.

Bless us with vision to perceive,
Contrive ideals for the future,
To be capable to persuade others
To join us in the quest for tomorrow.

Bless us with the realization
That life is not forever,
That no gorgeous penthouse
Will replace the little grave.

Bless us with the opportunity
To serve our families, community.
At the end of our days we will
Be able to say: "We have done our best."

September 30, 1984

Realization

"I cannot conceive: choose not to believe in Him who
having turned my body to fine ash begins once more to
wake me."

Aaron Zeitlin

In the heat of the Kara Kum desert
flames burst through my eyes, burning,
drying up every drop of hope.
I ran in fear, an immature child,
afraid to face sadness, pain.
From the shores of the Syr Daria
to the Vistula River, in profound grief
I buried my outrage and despair
when I saw those created
in Your Image crucified. Cremated bonepiles
used to fertilize the field.

Now I search for the earthly peace,
away from the torment I witnessed.
I need courage to see my own
unworthiness, not to choose scapegoats
to blame for my imperfections.
I do not run any more from human misery.
I stopped reproaching Heaven for earthly sin;
no more am I an island to myself,
though I have never seen my Heavenly Father,
I am able to feel His Presence.

Chrabrost — Courage!

Roses are planted where thorns grow,
And on the barren heath
Sing the honey bees.

William Blake

After nine months of misery, despair, near dead,
all the dread wounds over my body were healed.
They clothed me in a new Polish uniform, gave
me a pair of shoes, crutches, a travel permit
and directions to my military unit in Majdanek.
There was only one more important task to perform.

I dragged my feet to an office on an upper floor,
to say "thank you" to a woman who restored my life.
On the gray door was her name engraved on wood:
Valentina Ivanowna Korchukowa, Doctor of Medicine,
a simple note was attached to the metal door:
"We will win this war, all we need is courage!"

My feelings were stirred, bewildered, emotions
mixed. I was happy and sad, calm and worried;
For months I prayed, hoped to leave this place,
away from the smell of streptocide, carbolic acid.
I saw people losing arms, legs, dying in pain,
myself having a rough time, calling it H E L L.

I doubted if my limbs would ever function,
whether I would ever walk, ever talk again,
would my memory return? the constant bleeding
subside? I was twenty-five when brought in here,
now, I staggered up to this iron door, to thank
the woman, twice my age, I respected and admired.

This hard-working doctor, controlled my life,
often, when examining me, she cursed, shouted,
but always left my ward stirring my spirit with
a smile on her face and word: "Chrabrost!. . . .
Many times I cursed her, cried from pain from her
injections, for removing bandages too quickly

For her demands to move my toes, insulting me.
She called me S.O.B. I called her beast.
But for some reason, if I hadn't seen her a day
I was miserable, moaning, complaining, missing her. . .
When finally I was able to move my toes, she
summoned her staff to show them "a miracle."

Some nights she came to our ward, exhausted,
sat on the edge of our beds, quietly saying:
"I know the pain you all are bearing, the grief
and despair you're carrying, worrying who will
leave here without limbs, what future awaits you?
Will you be less the men you all dreamed of? . . .

"A rose can blossom near a stink hole, a pit,
flowers can scatter their fragrance at dirt piles,
what all of you here need is dew we call chrabrost
you need courage, will-power to endure, don't give in,
humans are like flowers, feed them with perseverence,
this is my prescription for your survival."

Casually she continued her words of comfort:
"People can live useful lives with one arm or leg
and make their contribution to the community.
Even a caterpillar, ugly, deaf and totally blind,
has its role on this earth, has its own purpose,
not every creature can fly, some of us just crawl.

But with patience, strength, determination, some of
us caterpillars will wake up as butterflies. . . .
Not everyone can grow to be a tall pine tree,
some of us must be satisfied to be a scrub, a lean
bush, or just low, green grass in a field. If you
can't be a doctor then serve as a medic. Do your duty!

There is work for all of us, regardless what we are,
some of us are leaders, some of us are followers.
Don't complain if you can't be a captain, a general
who controls the wide highways, masses of people,
be satisfied that you survived and can control
your own trail, your life, cheer up, courage!"

Now, leaving this hospital and this brave woman,
I realized how much Dr. Korchukowa did for me.
How much I admired and respected her all this time
I opened the heavy door, swallowing the tears,
I said quietly: "Spasibo Valentina Ivanowna."
She turned toward me, her face, clear and dear, smiled.

She squeezed my hand, grabbed me in her arms and
hugged me, I began to weep, sob loudly.
"Cheer up, Grisha, be a man, show some self control."
The tears streamed down on her white uniform,
"Get out of here you S.O.B. You made me cry. . .
Take good care of yourself, Wsio Choroshoho!"

This was January, Nineteen Forty-Five, in Europa;
now, four decades later, thousands of miles away,
I still remember this chubby, warm human being,
the doctor with always smiling, brown eyes, open
face. I still hear her commanding voice in my dreams;
"All that counts in life for survival is courage."

134

Teachers

We are often restless, tired, nervous,
worn out by the stress in the classroom.

Frequently we face the brink of despair,
ready to loose our temper and scream.

We clip our wings; bite our tongues,
not to show scorn for some unruly kid.

Yet, when the end of a semester comes,
we see that our work was not in vain.

Gloom disappears, satisfaction sets in,
when in solitude we read the class papers.

We see progress and feel triumphal joy
We praise our pupils and are proud of them.

The commendation of our endeared idols
are our own reassurance, self-congratulation.

A realization that the path we have chosen
was right. We look forward to the next season.

Poetic Notes

Not penned-down schedule reminders,
notes of what I have seen, heard
on certain dates, between the shadows

Not comments on how I feel about
people and happenings around me,
the turmoil and disorder in our days.

But reflections, sounds I hear from
a distance. Voices of songs that linger
deep in my soul for many decades.

Not the echoes of piano keys hit by
my fingers in a lonely moment,
but the humming voice of me singing inwardly.

A wailing sound like a siren in the night,
full of pain, anxiety, soundless lament,
calling, begging for attention, help.

A warning sign asking for remembrance:
A generation, an epoch, a people gone,
a precious past which I can't, I won't forget!

Poetic notes, windows into my soul.
You can see through and beyond
all that really matters to me.
I imagine myself addicted
to creating words, like a child
to her doll, her blanket.
Surely, there are other ways
to express my fondness and dislikes,
to bemoan the absurdity of war,
the profanation of God's name
at inaugurations of new bombs.
But my way to cry or laugh,

to reach the stars in heaven
or bring down God to earth
is by creating word cells
made of simple poetic notes.

MIRROR OF MEMORY

The Grocer on Warner Street

The shrill of sirens pierces the air,
dogs bark, cats weep all night.
Outside the bar across the street
drunkards sing and curse loudly.
He crawls under the cover, tries to sleep,
his five-year old daughter pulls his arm
crying; she is afraid of the dark,
does not want to sleep in her bed,
she is seeing monsters outside the window.
While her mother goes downstairs for milk
and a cookie, he tries to calm her:
"There is nothing to be scared of,
all the windows have iron bars."
He holds her in his arms and worries:
What takes her so long downstairs?. . .
The minutes seem like long hours,
he thinks of sharp pointed knives,
of someone hiding in a dark corner
behind the counter. . .Finally his wife
is back with milk and cookies,
his daughter is sound asleep on his chest.
Minutes later his tired wife snores. . .
He lies awake counting sirens,
listening to rats (or is someone again
trying to break in the back door?)
When he finally falls asleep,
the milkman and the bread truck ring:
Time to open the store. . . .

Baltimore, Md. 1951

141

Corner Myrtle and Lafayette

Invaders have beset the corner,
warrior-like thugs hanging around
undaunted, flagrantly displaying
knives, pistols, machetes; peddling
heroin, cocaine, drugs to captive
customers — blurred-eyed junkies,
who pay for their habit with
stolen welfare checks, goods in
shopping bags, not bothered by
a man who keeps vigil in a car.

The people are scared to sit on
the front porches of their houses,
afraid to let kids play outside.
They know that the harmless junkies
will, in a craze, kill for a dime
in desperation for a fix. . .
Myrtle and Lafayette, a landmark
for men with needle-poked veins,
possessive drug dealers, and police
who sit in cars and pretend blindness.

Every time I pass this corner
and see the numbed kids poised for a fix,
willing fools for the greedy dealers,
my heart trembles, beset with compassion
for their grieving, distressed mothers.
I feel despair, scorn for myself, for
being witness to crime and doing nothing.
I despise the man in the unmarked car
who, day after day, just sits there. . .
Our silence makes us accessories.

Baltimore, Md. March 1968

Rainbow

To a Montgomery County Policeman

"When the lamp is shattered,
The light in the dust lies dead;
When the cloud is scattered,
The rainbow's glory is shed."
Percy Bysshe Shelley

On a glorious, genial spring day in May,
the sky suddenly changed to darkness,
large pearl-drops started to fall
rhythmically, like silent tears and
changed into big showers.
A wailing wind came roaring from heaven,
pieces of roof tile, weeds scattered in
my yard, dispersed by the storm,
water runs indiscriminately, coming
from all directions, flooding
my kitchen and garage.
Thunder and lightning, falling
rain on my roof continues,
My neighbor's back yard looks like a lake,
on the far end of my street
cars swim in all directions.
The radio keeps warning Tornado Alert!
On the corner of Georgia and Bel-Pre Road
the traffic light went out.
Hot tempered people quarrel with
their car horns, drive irregularly,
An angel from heaven, a policeman
parks his car in front of my home
and in the midst of the raging storm
regulates the traffic. . .
The radio continues the tornado warnings,
talks of fallen trees, blown-off roofs,
The traffic light goes on,
the drenched policeman disappears,
the rain stops, my garden is gone,
just a hole in the ground,

my club room carpet is ruined,
my wife, daughter, myself work barefoot
to get the water out from the garage
still emerging from beneath the trees,
gushing with new power into the house,
but I keep thinking of an angel
in a policeman's uniform, regulating traffic
in the worst storm of the year
on the corner of Georgia and Bel-Pre
and in the back of him — a rainbow. . .

On Memorial Day

I sat beneath an oak tree
in the rear of my house,
holding a blank sheet of paper
on my lap, waiting for the muses.
I was gazing at the moon
the night light of G-d's garden,
inhaling cool air, aroma of grass,
mingled with the odor of
fried fish coming from my
neighbor's yard. The muses weren't
coming. . .I shut my eyes.
I let the wind take me on
the wings of my dreams
to places where phones don't ring,
no clocks to watch. . .
no newspapers to read
about violence, politics,
like a spider twine, the stillness
built a net around me,
I hear the trees whisper prayers,
the faint cry of crickets,
The green lawn under my feet
turns into a magic carpet,
like a lunatic I walk upwards
on this green carpet to the stars. . .
I was awakened by my wife
muttering from an upstairs window:
"Where are you? Are you asleep?
Come up and watch television."
I looked at the screen;
"Sheerest nonsense, I haven't missed
a great deal" I said.
"Certainly not," she answered,
"just that I want you in the house,
I want you to sit beside me. . . ."
My conscience felt guilty;
Here are we waiting for a day

of rest, to honor valor,
remember their spirit,
sacrifice for kin and country,
and here,
I'm flying to the stars,
waiting to write poetry-rhymes,
noticed the cry of crickets
and didn't see my lonely wife. . .
We fell asleep holding hands.

Deferred Poems

We are not now that strength which in old days
Moved earth and heaven, that which we are, we are, —
One equal temper of heroic hearts,
Made weak by time and fate, but strong in will
To strive, to seek, to find, and not to yield.
Alfred Lord Tennyson

When I retire,
I'll take vacations;
from mountainous Vermont
to sunny California,
visit friends in Minnesota,
lecture in Miami, Florida,
when I retire.

When I retire,
I'll fly to Kfar Sava,
visit my grandchildren,
stop off at relatives,
climb Mount Hermon,
sunbathe in Eilat,
when I retire.

When I retire,
I will study in Jerusalem,
take dirt-baths in Tiberias,
pray at the tombs of
Rabbi Meir Baal Haness
and Reb Shimon Bar Yochai,
when I retire.

Upon return from my voyages,
I'll write poems, essays:
"How good it is to be back home."
I'll teach, lecture on Yiddish,
join a health club, exercise,
will try to lose weight,
when I retire.

When I retire,
I will work for my favorite
charities: UJAF, BJE, ORT,
Yad Va'Shem. Maybe I will
finish my dissertation on
"How to lead an active life."
If I'll live so long to retire. . . .

January 31, 1982

After the Storm

A calm day, frigid weather,
neither wind or snow-drifts.
A gray heaven like a block
of metallic lead clouds the sky.
In the safety of our homes
we sit and watch television:
a woman struggling against nature
in the murky Potomac River,
firemen carrying people on stretchers,
a man tangled in the icy river,
the shambles of cars on the bridge.

We watch how heroes are born:
Lenny Skutnick jumps into the Potomac
to save a drowning woman's life.
We think of the victims, their dreams,
did they suffer when dying?
We think of God, fate, destiny,
the fragility of human lives.
The only spark of sunshine
in this gloomy, cloudy week
is the face of Lenny Skutnick:
He conquered the icy river.
The harsh tragedy had a touch
of an epic: A miracle scene
of genuine courage.

I arose this morning to the sound
of water flowing down the roof,
The skies look gloomy, like mourners
dressed in dark cloud-rags.
There is no more wind, not the
slightest flutter of the trees.
The rain sounds like a quiet sobbing,
with the tears dropping

making dimples on the white frozen snow.
The rain and sleet fit my mood.
The faces of the dazed, blinded victims
in the muddy Potomac, follow me.
This morning they discovered the body
of a child of three months.
Something in me weeps like the rain
outside my window.

January 25, 1982

On a Foggy Day

A wren sits motionless
on a naked branch,
the tree looks like
an open, upward coffin
placed on a white
tablecloth, the icy mist.
I walk zigzag in the snow,
a foot deep, taking bread crumbs
for the wren that sits
unmoved on a branch.
A vast shadow of cloud
rests beneath my windows,
the whole sky falls down
and clings to the roof,
the quiet fog hovers
over the tree in my yard,
where the wren sits
calm, cold, motionless.
I watch in silence
the heavy, gray clouds,
the bread crumbs I spread
on the yard table, and
the wren that sits unstirring
on the naked branch.
I stare with pity at
this lonely bird; the waiting
makes me sad and nervous.
Finally, the wren flies
to the table. I can't
describe how happy I am.
But, too late. . . .a squirrel
comes leaping from the woods,
and in a split of a moment
devours the bread crumbs.
By the time I get back
with more challa crust
the wren is gone. . . .

February 1982

Fall. . .

The leaves on my dogwood tree
have turned red, a bleeding color,
like the evening sun in the sky.

The dying leaves are strewn
over the grass; they remind me
of life's twilight: how years die.

How our hair changes colors,
how our longings dissolve —
melt in the splendor of fall.

I know my dogwood tree will bloom,
new leaves will blossom in spring,
birds will dwell on her branches.

The marigolds, violets and lilies,
as in the past springs and summers,
will flourish until next fall.

I only wonder, will I be still here
to see the bursting roses, tulips,
to hear the voice of birds and bees.

But spring is far away, a long wait;
clouds, ice, wind and snow must pass
before my dogwood tree will bloom.

Let's celebrate the festival of fall;
there is beauty in the golden leaves,
as in the softness of golden years.

October 28, 1982

A Perception of Human Nothingness

A whistling wind makes patterns of clouds
look like floating ships adrift in the sky,
loaded with the faces of demons and angels:
The flowers at my bedside smell of disinfectants
from the water that my nurse, a double-chinned
pious-faced, full-bosomed matron, put them in.

Naked trees through the snow-covered window
look like my reflection, a shadow of pale gray.
I have an urge to leave the warmth of this room,
the friendly nurse, the flowers, get-well cards,
and escape from this snow-white bed into the yard,
to embrace the naked trees, breathe the cool air,
to keep walking, running until I collapse at
the door-steps of my home, miles away from here. . .

Trembling hands pick me up, take me back to my room,
but too late. . .My soul has departed from my body.
A quorum of adults pray at my deathbed, while
the double-chinned nurse with the pious face
washes my forehead with beaten eggs and wine,
dresses my body in my Passover Kittel — a garment
made of white linen with unknotted thread. . .

I awaken shivering, gazing at the flowers,
the trees outside which look like me, without skin.
I feel terrible, unbelievably tired, my nerves frayed,
the pain in my back intense and persistent:
the shrouds, the praying quorum were only a dream. . .
deep inside me I feel a degree of happiness. . .
Here comes the matron-nurse with a needle,
what a joy to hear her commanding voice!. . .

Sibley Hospital, April 1979

153

One Day

On Sunday morning
I like to get up early,
repose in a chair
at my kitchen window,
observe busy birds
searching for food.
Today I noticed a spider
weaving a web outside
the window frame,
squirrels chasing
up and down the oak tree.
I sit at the window
listening to the news,
inhaling the cool air,
water pearls cover
the green leaves
like tiny light bulbs —
reflections from the sun.
From the distance
an ambulance pierces the air,
the barking of a dog
disturbs the quietness.
The birds continue their
search for daily sustenance,
the spider is still spinning.
I can't stop thinking
of that ambulance shrill;
A person is facing death,
here the sun is shining,
birds sing, squirrels play
and I, selfishly, enjoy the
tranquility of a Sunday morning.

Evening, no birds sing,
safe and sound they sleep.
The night is cool
the branches on the trees
swaying back and forth.
I look out the window,
and cannot help thinking
of the ambulance which
disrupted the morning quiet.
Is the patient alive, or dying?
or, was it a woman in labor pains
rushing to bring forth a new life?

Lunchtime in the Capitol City

Opposite the White House,
a vagabond on a park bench
is eating watermelon peel,
sharing his feast with pigeons
who pick seeds off his hand.
He searches in the nearby
trash-container for dessert,
finds a beer can and squeezes
out of it one last drop.
People stroll by leisurely
enjoy fresh air, shining sun.
All park benches are occupied
except for the bench where
the peculiar hobo is having
his feast of watermelon rind
and pigeons eating of his hand. . .

Too Busy

"What is this life if, full of care,
We have no time to stand and stare."
W. H. Davies

Only a Solomon could understand
the twittering of swallows.
We mortals are too busy
to hear the chirping
of mockingbirds engaged in
morning games.

Pity, we are up to our ears
every morning shaving, showering,
brushing teeth, eating cereal,
reading newspapers, rushing to work,
no time left to watch
how birds spread their wings
hovering over their sweethearts.
Were we not too busy,
we could learn something from birds
being free. . .without waiting
for the resurrection of Solomon. . . .

July 1978

To The Readers

My verses can accomplish wonders:
Blend beauty with ugliness,
peace with war, love with hate,
trust with fear, birth with death.

I can turn despots into slaves,
change mortals into angels.
I can lift low spirits from despair
to hope, from the verge of doom
to high heaven, make beggars into kings.

I am a magician, witch and prophet;
I can make trees bloom in winter,
plants, flowers grow in desert sand
find water in split rocks. Find God
in the darkest place of torment,
walk out from hell into paradise.

I can make you sing when you feel sad,
find a spark of light in darkness.
I can take you on a magic carpet,
lift you over mountains and oceans
and show you the world's beauty. . . .
But you, the reader, must decide.
Fling the poems aside with scorn,
or let your fantasy float with me,
to blend your dreams with my poems. . . .

A Visitor

To my grandchildren

My father died when I was four.
I remember his face from pictures,
in an album with satin covers.
My mother used to turn the pages
for me, some five decades ago.
Last night, Thanksgiving Eve,
after my children and guests left,
I was dozing in my armchair,
when the door opened and my father
came in. We recognized each other
immediately. I got up to greet him:
"Here are you at last, I've been waiting,
yearning for you for so long.
Sorry you did not come a while ago,
to see your grandchildren here."
"Father," I said, "Susi and I are blessed
with a precious gift. Look at the pictures
of our children in this living room."
"Listen, son, pictures on walls are
only images. If your children will carry
your picture in their hearts
as you carried mine, then you have
children and they have a father."
I wanted to ask him quite seriously
what he was trying to tell me,
but my granddaughter Shelly
pulled my sleeve excitedly:
"Grandpa. You promised me a story."
Evidently, I was dreaming; still,
I was deeply shaken by my father's visit.
I told my Shelly a story of a father,
who came to visit his son, after
five decades and five thousand miles away.

November 1977

159

Grandfather

It is not thinking with the primitive ingenuity of
childhood that is most difficult, but to think with
tradition, with its acquired force and with all the
accumulated wealth of its thought.

Auguste Rodin

The older I get the more I feel,
think like you throughout.
The same Covenant that bound
you to God is the vitalizing
power that protects me today.
My experiences will never be
quite the same as yours.
Exceptions: a missing beard,
a velvet skullcap. . .I don't
observe traditional requirements.
Nevertheless, your sense of humility,
hospitality to the stranger,
basic common humanity is growing
in me, body and soul.
My heart is longing for the spirit
of your chassidic "shtibel,"
with no fancy chazonim and choirs,
no fancy hypocritic sermons,
a place where we prayed inwardly. . .

There was always place at our table
for a hungry stranger for Shabbat.
Now, on Friday Eve, I make Kiddush
using your nigun — your melody.
I think that even my voice
sounds more and more like yours. . .

At Sixty Six

I am still terrified by the grief of the past,
but age granted me an abundance of tranquility.

I learned to derive pleasure from little things:
A friendly greeting, a smile from my grandchildren.

My thoughts are mocked by memories of a violent
war, physical pain, spiritual tumult and endless pain.

But the conditions of my survival are so unusual
that despite all disappointments I still believe in God.

My senses travel between grief and pleasure,
between love for my friends and compassion for enemies.

Age made my body frail, more humble at sixty-six,
everything from the past looks profoundly insignificant.

What matters now is how can I serve humanity,
my people, in the remaining days. . . .

To Aaron

I applaud your many skills,
I am proud of your talent —
to paint, to act, to swim.
Someday you're going to be
a virtuoso, an inventor of
some gadget that will make
you famous and rich. . . .
What I wish for you is
something more simple:
Strength of character,
honesty, personal integrity.
Don't lose your identity,
the quality of originality,
however humble, still to be
proud of: Look at your parents:
I'm not flattering them,
but, you must admit, they are
loyal, honest, caring parents.

If you really want to paint,
sketch me a bold eagle,
with his wings spread wide,
flying in the sky, free and high
above mountains and forests,
with his eyes looking down,
trying to discover the earth's secrets,
looking from a distance for space
to build his own, secure nest.
When you finish the drawing,
you will realize that you have captured
on canvas your grandfather's image
and dreams of you. . . .

January 1982

Rainstorm

A roaring wind, menacing the flowers,
hits my yard suddenly with rage,
a rainstorm blows violence, drowning
my garden, windbeating the tomato plants.

I walk restlessly from room to room
conversing with pictures on walls;
the house is deserted like the street
which is swollen with a tide of dirty water.

My hungry typewriter is waiting for
its daily workout, but fingers get stiff.
I'm in a stupor, overwhelmed by the downpour,
not knowing what to think or what to write.

The clouds look mean, dark on the horizon,
the stream sweeps away the flowers.
My fantasy follows the wild current,
imagination flows with the wave; I'm drifting:

I see myself on a steamboat, sailing
the coast of Natanya, Israel.
A storm forces our crew to land
on a beach with throngs of people.

A little girl comes running, shouting,
"What a surprise! look who is here?"
She lifts her arms, presses to my chest,
her eyes are searching, "Where is Grandma?"

From a nearby playground a little boy
moves toward me holding a toy truck,
looks at silly me holding back the tears.
He asks, "Where are Judy, Bob, Myron?"...

The doorbell interrupts my daydream,
Yes, there is a letter from my children.
I feel like kissing the soaked mailman,
but he disappeared in the flooded street.

The rainstorm continues, wind blows,
knocks down trees; my yard is a swamp.
I read and enjoy my daughter's handwriting.
Everything inside begins to sing.

Monday, August 27, 1979

The Dove

(autobiographically speaking. . .)

Taube'n, doves, are as old as humanity.
We can be found on all continents;
we come in different breeds, colors,
possess courage, intelligence, humility.

Some of us wear crowns, look aristocratic,
are of rare beauty, like the dancing Fawtail;
others, artists of great talent like the Tumblins,
famous for their stunts and acrobatics.

There are also among us silly clowns,
very lazy birds who live on handouts in parks,
boulevards, eat crumbs off pavements
instead of looking for grass and grain.

We are vigorous travelers who fly far
distances, but always find our way back home.
Because we are gentle, soft-spoken, friendly,
we were chosen as the world's symbol of peace.

We love life, like to eat and drink a lot,
don't care about fancy homes: Any structure
will satisfy us as long as it protects from wind
our affectionate devoted mates and brood.

For generations, voracious birds have hunted us,
mischievous boys chase us with slingshots,
trap us in cages, enslave and annihilate us,
but claim that they are our friends, guardians.

After our "protectors" slaughter our kind
they praise our qualities and characteristics;
how good and tender we taste fried or roasted,
how humble and kind we were up to the last.

165

Despite all predators we have survived,
we traveled with Noah during the great flood
and "saw all flesh perish, blotted out from earth."
Our names are inscribed in history books.

In Noah's ark, among beasts, fowl, creeping things,
we learned not to discriminate against others.
When the Ark reached the shores of A R A R A T
one of us was chosen to carry the olive leaf.

When you see us in a park do you wonder
why we make chirping sounds around you?
We learned not to take life for granted,
we are murmuring our daily prayers.

October 22, 1979

To My Children

. . .at the end
of the road,
when life
will wash away
last dreams,
I will say
goodby to you
and ask for
a last favor.
Plant flowers
in my yard;
roses, tulips,
chrysanthemums.
On holidays,
anniversaries,
set a cluster
on your table
and quietly say·
"Remember him."

Possibly,
(if you desire)
light a candle
on my "yartzeit,"
the lit wick
is not just
for me alone;
it's for all
my loved family,
all our people
who perished
and did not
leave children
or relatives

to remember them
on observance days.
The shine of
the small flame
gleaming on
your table.

My Grandfather's View...

My grandfather's life pattern
was prayer, study, good deeds.
One custom he objected to:
the inferior status of women.
He admired, loved my grandmother,
was proud of his four daughters,
educating them in private schools
comparing them with Rashi's daughters.
On Sukkoth holiday, he insisted
that grandmother and my aunts
join him in the sukkah festival
singing zmiroth songs until midnight!...
He called grandma "Eyshes Chayil"
selfless like Rachel, Rabbi Akiba's wife.
Contrary to customary manners,
he insisted that my grandmother
walk beside him instead of in back...
I remember him saying: "Your mother
does not need false compliments,
but don't make her your servant,
treat her with respect and esteem.
A woman is a 'mentsch' like you.
Yochevet and Miriam raised a Moses....
Mothers are the heart of the family,
don't fool around with the heart!"

Waiting

To Miriam, Shelly and Danny

The home scrubbed,
the bathroom cleaned,
beds straightened up
with fresh bedspreads
the house is waiting
for my children's arrival.

I sit in a happy mood
at the living-room window,
inhale the early morning air
enjoy the blue, clear sky,
while bits of memories
pass through my mind.

In moments of loneliness
I feel safety at this window,
watching mating birds play,
But today I'm full of emotions,
my mind, my ears on alert
for the door-bell to ring. . .

A year of longing passed,
now, any moment, at last
I will hold them in my arms,
G-d! How slow the clock moves,
I can't wait to see their faces,
hear their tales, singing, laughing.

I hear my car in the yard,
I pretend to be calm,
my heart beats with joy,
my hands are trembling,
my eyes are filled with tears;
Shalom! Welcome Home!

Death

Metaphor for nothingness,
description of eternal peace,
one way ticket to nowhere;
an awaited tourist-package
with guaranteed arrival
for those who cast stones
for those who work splitting stones
with chisel and mallet,
for those who write songs and chant
them to those who live in dark corners.
An equal-opportunity employer
who receives evenhandedly
the cobbler and the king;
the fortune-scion and common man.
The ones who die for a cause
and the ones who perish because
of a cause. . .Those who live in palaces
with their iron doors shut,
those farmers with their dungforks,
maids with their sloppails,
field workers in the sun;
they will all arrive,
the meek, strong, bad, noble, sinner or saint,
the glorified, downtrodden,
learned, famous, or forgotten.
All arrive at the same destination;
the court of eternal truth.

Contrast

Tomblike monsters of iron, concrete, glass
look down on moving, hurrying masses.
Subway trains vibrate under my feet,
make my body shiver, my knees shake.

A sea of glimmering neon signs attack,
blind my vision with their glowing light.
The sound of horns, music, loud voices
pierces my auricles, silences my hearing.

I am startled by the towers of Babel,
skyscrapers, wonders of architecture,
like the human mind trying, desiring
to reach the entrance of the firmament.

I am frightened by the dissonance of faces,
walking, standing on Broadway and Forty-Second:
winos, pimps, prostitutes, shady characters
among a mass of friendly smiling people.

I see the contrast between the genius
human mind, creators of technical wonders,
and the fragility, nothingness of human nature
unable to cope with the rhythm of life.

I feel small, lonely, strange among this crowd.
Wind and rain hit the enormous buildings;
the heavens lower themselves to the rooftops
ready to carry off the masses to the sea.

I wonder if I will disappear in the atmosphere
like a drop of rain on the roofs above me.
Will I be missed by someone? The crowd, like rain
no one notices when it evaporates. . . .

New York, August 1976

172

On the S.S. Rotterdam

Two people holding hands
stroll on the shipdeck
in early morning hour,
when the sun is still
sleeping, hiding under clouds;
the wind is battering
their faces with rain.
Undisturbed by the rugged ocean,
they walk smiling at each other,
two faces full of joy.
They inhale the fresh air,
the coolness and tranquillity
of this great ship's upper deck.
With tenderness he stretches out
his arms, throws them around
her shoulders. The noise of waves,
the silence of missing crowds,
fills the morning with warmth,
though the rain reaches their bones.
Kissing her forehead, he remarks:
"Love knows no time, no season. . . ."

S.S. Rotterdam, August 8, 1978

Marriage

"Enter into every man's ruling reason,
and give every one else an opportunity
to enter into thine."

Marcus Aurelius

Lately, I sleep a lot;
sometimes I pretend to doze,
a self-hypnosis that does
not see reality.
My youngest child is getting married.
The weeks are slipping away,
the day is near when my Judy,
in a bride's gown and veil,
will stay under a chuppa
decorated with flowers, among
a crowd of guests, relatives,
like in a contrived play.
She will whisper: "I do!"
I will be part of the ceremony,
smile to well-wishers,
be kissed in the reception line
by total strangers, who will
spontaneously embrace me, smile,
shake my hands to wish "Mazal Tov"
and shower us with compliments:
"Isn't she charming! Pu-Pu-Pu.". . .
My heart feels like it is being
plundered of something precious;
my priceless treasure is being
taken from me in a ritual,
with the rabbi's blessing.
I am too poor to relinquish it,
too weak to resist: She is so happy. . . .

Lean Days. . .

Lean days.
A reaction that followed
Judy's wedding,
an emotional let down,
completely devoid of
lucid visions, images;
no fascinating stories
leaping up in the
fountain of my mind.
The big house
suddenly looks empty, small.
All I can think of is
Judy is moving out,
all I can see is
Judy's empty bed.
Total immobility,
I don't even try to write,
I walk around the house
like a shadow.
If all of this is not enough,
I face one more jolt;
tomorrow Shelly, Danny and Miriam
will leave. G-d knows when
again I will see them.
It is agonizing
not to let emotions show
when facing children's departure. . .

August 14, 1979

175

My Yard

I love my back yard,
solitary birds sitting motionlessly
on my garage window,
the barking of my neighbor's dog,
the squirrels running wild
on the broken rocks and trees.
Summertime mornings I like
the smell of fresh hay, after
the grass is cut and sparkles
in the morning breeze that
flicker the bushes and trees.
Before leaving for work
I lift a toast to heaven
for the sunlight and the grass.
Evenings, when I return home,
the sun, a red ball, comes down
slowly darkening my yard.
A crouching windy chill
crawls through the grass;
the wind blows in my face.

June 2, 1983

We Are Cowards

We are cowards, ashamed to cry out loud
when tears are ready to burst:
we don't attend The Vigil often enough
to show how much we care, remember.
Our excuse: Too busy making a living.

We are cowards, hiding in shells,
afraid to show madness when anger is ready
to explode for the hate unleashed upon
our brethren in lands of oppression.
Our excuse: They are not in mortal danger.

We are cowards, extravagant with words,
stingy in action, more a crowd than
an organized community. Mediocrity reflects in our actions;
we shout: Let Our People Go! and are too tired
to practice what we preach, to show concern.

We are cowards, silent to the sufferings
of freedom fighters, activists, 'refuseniks.'
When we see onrushing forces of a ruthless
enemy blotting out our culture, heritage,
there can be no excuse for being silent!

At Babi Yar

Yet I, whose lids from infant slumber
Were earlier raised, remain to hear
A timid voice, that asks in whispers,
"Who next will drop and disappear?"

William Wordsworth

A casual sigh of a solitary survivor;
An urge to carry his fate, cruel past
Brings him here to the ravine.
Afraid to be seen or heard, he prays
In whispers, eyes glowing with fright.
In the morning fog he sees a silhouette,
A man in military uniform walking toward him.
He is afraid of his shadow, his lips stop moving,
His whole body shakes with worry.
The officer stops, looks at his face
And with a voice breaking, begging:
"Diadushka, would you know how to say Kaddish?
I lost my parents here in September '41,
While I was away fighting in the war."

While on the outside world they're denying
That the Jews of Kiev ever existed,
And Babi Yar never ever happened,
A man in autumn of his years and a broad-
shouldered soldier — a child of martyrs —
Continue a ritual of remembrance.
The morning fog hangs over Babi Yar.
A bird twitters on the monument top.
Two shadows with sagging, swaying shoulders
Repeat in unison: "Yisgadal V'Yiskadash!"

Taking Chances

Today I planted four Norway spruces.
I wondered if I am not too late
to plant in July, when the grass
in my yard is drying,
the sky hot and humid.
Yet, I decided to take a chance.

This week I am leaving for Israel,
to plant some knowledge in my old head.
I wonder if I am not too late
in the autumn of my years
to travel such long distances,
to miss my wife's laughter, my
children's voices and grandchildren's
merry faces; they are the spark
that gives worth to my life. . . .

The ground was stone dry
and I planted four Norway spruces.
The plane flight gnaws at my mind.
nibbling my nerves with worries.
Still, I decided to take the
chance and go.

November Winds. . .

I was awakened this morning
by an autumn wind whistling
on my roof and windows.
It was early dawn, too late
to go back to sleep. I walked
around the house, inhaling
the fresh-painted odor of
the four empty bedrooms.
Looking at the pictures of
my children I remembered
holidays, family feasts,
loud music and songs by
Elvis, Sinatra and the Beatles,
phones ringing past midnight,
happy chatter, laughter, songs.
now everything faded away,
the children gone their way.
The house looks like an oversized
box, the warmth gone,
the paintings look out of place,
like my daughters' wedding gowns
still hanging in our closets.
I suddenly feel cold and return
to our bed. Susi, still drowsy,
half asleep, crawls into my arms:
"Why are you up so early?". . .
Outside my windowpane the wind
is moaning, it doesn't matter now,
Susi's warm breath is on
my chest, she is part of me.

Nov. 4, 1983

A Sign of Spring

In the back of my home
I see a robin
on my naked oak tree.
The dogwood bud responds
to the warmth of the sun
unfolding bracts, red oak
comes alive. On the old
winter leaves a mushroom appears
Wild geraniums blossom —
I start sneezing,
my eyes start itching.
I know spring is here
in all her glory. . . .

JOURNEY AHEAD

The World Gathering

We meet at Kennedy Airport,
express our feelings in hugging,
seeing friends, landsleit
we haven't heard of in decades.

Faces with marks of age and pain,
signs of battle to survive the war
and the aftermath of liberation,
we greet each other in silence.

Words, speeches are not needed;
Our eyes talk with tears,
long repressed emotions, longings,
pour out our love for each other.

Uppermost for Israel, for Jerusalem;
we are going there to demonstrate
for life, for strengthening our bonds:
sharing our inheritance with our children.

We talk about the price Israel paid
with the lives of her sons, daughters,
to make it possible for us survivors
to go there without restrictions. . . .

To walk the streets of Jerusalem
with our heads up and steps secure,
celebrating life, saying: Mir Zenen Do!
Let the world know: We Are Here!

Our plane flies over mountains, highlands,
oceans, skies, on a chartered course.
Destination: Lod, Ben Gurion Airport.
Weary travelers keep their eyes closed.

Who knows what chapter of life they recount
beyond their closed eyelids? in their sleep?
They all had their share of tragedy, struggle,
in the painful, perilous years.

They did not flinch in face of danger,
courageously resisted despair, apathy,
their faces, wrinkled, still express courage,
a mixture of sad and jovial moods.

I don't know from where they are coming,
but I feel a deep kinship for all of them;
they are my people — survivors.
We are going to Jerusalem to Remember!. . .

On an Ancient Road

Jericho and Wadi Kelt lie behind us
with tumbled walls of a refugee camp.
We climb desolate hills to the top
of mountains on a stony, dry road
in the Judean hills, greeted by
black, hairy, astonished-looking goats.

On the high cliff we enjoy the view
of the barren desert, the cool, clear air.
Down in the oasis below we see the
ancient Greek Monastery of Forty Days
carved into the Mount of Temptation.
Wc feel the spirit of Joshua is with us.

The Rabbi tells the story
of this ancient road, the shrine, Jericho,
the prophets Elijah and Elisha.
We admire water streams built by Herod
running from the mountains to the oasis,
watering a variety of tropical species.

The bus driver calls, no one wants to leave.
It is so beautiful here. The cloudless sky
hugging, embracing the mountain top, and us. . . .
The architects among us dream: Build here
a "Tower of Babel," a "Palace of Peace" for
all Nations, to reach the entrance of heaven.

God, the angels seem just at arm's length. . . .
Our David blows the Tekkiah Gedolah,.
the tone of the shofar resounds in the hills.
We say Shalom to Joshua's spirit, the mountains,
return to the bus on our journey to Jerusalem.
Long-lost children returning to Mother Zion!. . . .

To Jerusalem

"All other cities performed great
circuits in the arena of time,
won or lost and died. .
Jerusalem stayed in her crouching-start:
all victories are coiled and hidden in her. All defeats."

Yehuda Amichai

From the mountains
of Beth El and Hebron
a cool breeze meets us.
From the Judean desert
a sun in full heat
welcomes us in.
From the ravines, valleys,
the canyons of Judea,
the souls of our ancestors,
of generations past,
receive us with their
holy, ancient spell.
A feeling that we were
here once before,
that our souls belong.
We, survivors of
Six Million Akedas
bring ourselves
and our children
to the altar of Jerusalem.
We pray together with
your inhabitants
that forever your name
by synonymous with peace.
To the many names
you are known by: Urusalim,
Yrushlym, Salem, Zion,
Hurosolima, City of David,
City of Justice,
We will add one more name:

Ingathering City of
the Shaarit Hapleita,
where the dry bones
came back to life
and proclaimed Jerusalem
God's City forever

Jerusalem Sabbath

To Rabbi Stanley Rabinowitz

"There is no beauty
like the beauty of Jerusalem."
The Fathers Ch. 28

I
From the window
of the Plaza Hotel
the ancient city looks
like my Zeyda — Olov Hasholom —
coming home from "mikve"
on Fridays,
serene, old, clean,
with Sabbath spirit
on his face.

The sun sets
for her night rest,
right behind palm trees
and the towers
of the Heichal Shlomo.
No cars, no noise,
just people of all ages
stroll the street below.
I want to stay here
all night, feel autumn air,
enjoy the ancient soothing
of Jerusalem.

But a vision
from the past,
my Zeyde, serene, old, clean
like the countenance
of this Sacred City,
with eyes sparkling,
greets me with "Gut Shabbes,
Sholom Aleychem, grandson,

time to go to The Wall;
Sabbath is descending,
time to greet Queen Shabbat."

II
Dressed in Divine Spirit,
the Sabbath Queen descends
from Judean Hills,
hovers over the City,
an "Additional Soul."
Longing pulls me
with overwhelming force,
like a magnetic flux,
to the unseen bridge
to the heart of God:
The Western Wall.

Faces, silhouettes, move
beside me, their attire
a rainbow of color,
a variety of plants
in an ancient forest.
Familiar melodies
overflow the air,
a blend of dialects
infused in one chant:
"The Lord will give
strength to his people."

We close our eyes.
Touching The Wall,
outpouring our hearts
with a fountain of tears.
We find tranquillity
of soul, feel lifted

to a sphere of joy,
solemnity of Sabbath.
We pray: "The Lord Will Bless
His People With Peace!"

This Crowd is Ours,
This Place is Mine. . .

We walk, holding hands,
with no map at our disposal.
Guided by common sense,
we find ourselves strolling
in the midst of unknown
alleys, narrow streets.
We feel strange, but not frightened
by the sight of Arabs.
We encounter nuns, a priest,
Scandinavian pilgrims climbing
steps to a church on the hilltop.
We keep going down, following
Arabs prodding overloaded donkeys,
children huddled together,
clutching their school books.
We walk in silence, listening
to the sound of church bells,
to the wailing of the muezzin,
coming from the minaret of a mosque.
This is not our song, we feel cold,
we are different, stagnant.
This is not our crowd.

We reach steps and see the Wall;
we observe men digging in a quarry,
excavating stones, pottery, millennia old.
History looks real here,
reality - like a fairy-tale.
The entrance to the Wall grounds,
the cradle of our faith,
is a market place for hucksters
selling yarmulkas, slides of
the Holy Sepulcher, the Omar Mosque,
beggars with outstretched palms. . . .
We can't explain the reason,

193

why the sight of the Wall
makes us feel so secure, at home. . . .
A new rhythm, a song comes up
deep from our hearts. . . .
The area is crammed with people,
natives, tourists from all over the globe.
The noise of their praying, singing,
overtakes the wailing of the muezzin.
A breath of Jerusalem's air
enters our souls: We cry and we smile.
People smile back, this crowd is ours,
this place is mine!

Jerusalem, June 1981

The Wall

"Being a Jew means running forever to God
Even if you are His betrayer,
Means expecting to hear any day,
Even if you are a nay sayer,
The blare of Messiah's horn."

Aaron Zeitlin

Prepossessed with thoughts
of ghetto walls, barbed wire,
images still lingering in
subconsciousness of Warsaw,
Crakow, Auschwitz-Birkenau,
like open scars, painful wounds,
my troubled, grieving soul
longed for peace of mind.
Driven by emotions, I walked
side by side with people
of all shades, denominations,
the path on the way to the Western Wall.

My eyes were fascinated
by the Dome of the Rock;
my ears listened to the ring
of bells from the Holy Sepulcher.
Yet my heart was drawn to The Wall.
Magnetic power must be hidden
in the texture of the stones.
I wondered why people beat
their breasts while praying.
It seems ridiculous for
grown men and women to talk to
ancient, cold stones. However,
I was pulled by the magnetic power.

I discovered a spot, reserved,
just waiting for me alone.
Suddenly, The Wall, me, we touched
each other. It is difficult

to believe how tears can come
bursting like a flash of lightning
unexpectedly, all by themselves. . . .

I did not feel embarrassed
to cry, pray out loud:
"Merciful God. Overwhelm my mind
with compassion for people.
Defeat the grudge I carry
against the enemies who hurt us.
Banish the hatred, bitterness,
wrath I bear. Help me disburden
the evil mood of Auschwitz,
the Umschlagplatz — wall of
Ghetto Warsaw, still transgressing,
holding firm my soul. . . ."
The Wall was silent, calm, tranquil.
A light of blinding brightness
reflected from the stones.
A warm soothing feeling of relief
passed over me. A new kinship reborn
between the stones, people and me.
In the rays of twilight I found peace.

World Gathering
Last Night at The Wall

"In the name of Allah,
the compassionate, the merciful.
Praise be to Allah,
Lord of the Universe,
the compassionate, the merciful.
Master of the Judgment Day."
I heard this chanting
all during our last event
at the Wall in Jerusalem,
at the World Gathering:
The Muezzin's chant
continued during the
memorial service, during
the reading of the Testament,
during Menachem Begin's
outcry: "What did they do
to a million Jewish children?"
During the blowing of shofarim
by barefoot Yemenites.
The only thing that sounded
stronger, more convincing
than the Mohammedan credo
was to the deep rich voice of
Benjamin Meed:
"Dos Yiddishe Folk Lebt!
Mir Zainen Do."
On the way back from the Wall
Arabs closed in on us.
For a moment I felt a stranger
in their midst.
I walked by, proud and tall.

They simply stepped aside.
No, I am not a stranger here.
This place is part of us, of me.
Mir Zainen Do! I kept repeating.
They didn't understand exactly
what I was saying,
but they simply fell back. . . .

Jerusalem, June 1981

Elie Wiesel Speaks. . .

You speak the language of my soul.
Your writings were at first a cry
of protest against the vulgarity of
silence and the indifference of our world
to the "Dawn" and "Night" of our century.

I followed you from Buchenwald to
Paris, to Moskow, to Jerusalem. I feel
at home in your Sighet as in Lodz.
I am the Silent Jew, the Madman and
the Beggar widely using your books.

I carry the Legend of our Days,
semester after semester, years now,
to my students, young and old.
You, Dear Elie, are our mystical
legend: Our conscience, our voice!

I heard you speak so many times:
in the White House in Washington,
at synagogues, college lectures,
at UJA events and conferences, and
at our World Gathering in Jerusalem.

But, never, did I feel so close
to you as this Tuesday morning in June,
at Kibbutz Lochamei HaGettaot,
when you spoke to us in the open field
in front of the Yitzhak Katzenelson Museum.

A light wind was carrying your voice,
warm, and simple, dignified and stimulating.
The clarity with which you shared
your thoughts, the ideals you instilled
in our minds gave me great satisfaction.

Even your gestures, facial expressions,
the tone of your voice, your hand and
body movements when you kept stroking,
straightening your hair, gave us pleasure.
Your presentation attested to our survival.

The World Gathering is now just a memory,
Long-buried hopes and fantasies erupted
in Jerusalem; we had the courage to unburden
our feelings and renew our loyalty oath to
the memory of our martyrs and heroes.

But I will go on remembering your voice,
as difficult and painful as the visit to
the Kibbutz was for me, seeing for the
last time the legendary Yitzhak Zuckerman,
Olov Hasholom,
I will cherish this day forever!

Lochamei HaGettaot. June 16, 1981

After the World Gathering

After four days
of smiles and hugs,
fusion of the old
with the new generation,
some fictitious,
mostly superficial. . . .
After blending joy
with unmanageable tears,
the past united us
and still left us lonely.
After hours of self-torment
with memorial prayers,
bringing back past fears,
nurturing false dreams:
"Universality of mankind
Common brotherhood,
Centrality of Israel
for our future survival."
Proclamations, speeches
left a hollow feeling,
a mood we can't shake:
We're still alone
in this world. . . .

After innumerable
cantorial chants,
voices of survivors
searching for lost kin,
all that remains is
a question in a vacuum:
What next? What future?
Daily realities play
hide and seek with us.
By day we struggle
to go on living, working,

providing for our needs.
At muggy nights
the World Gathering
comes back in our dreams,
like little peep-shows,
like the slides on
the roof of Yad Va'Shem.
At the opening ceremony,
we see the Wall, the flags,
the burning Yahrzeit candles,
the visages of Wiesel, Meed,
Michel, Begin's Lament:
"Why did they murder our
Kinderlach?"

Often I think of
the remarks by Pissar,
Arad, Hausner, Navon:
Accusing, demanding
answers, explanations.
I hear the sounding of
shofars by barefoot
Yemenites, reminding us
of our roots and
the Shofar Shel Moshi'ach. . . .
I see faces: so far,
and still so dear:
Norbert Wollheim,
Kalman Sultanik,
Vladke and Ben Meed
and their family.
Sam Mozes, James Rapp,
Ben Abraham from Brazil,
Konrad Charmatz, Sao Paulo,
Miriam Lazarus, Johannesburg,
and my dear friend
Yitzhak Zuckerman, Olov HaSholom. . .

My fellow survivors
from Washington,
Baltimore, Atlanta,
Cleveland, and Milwaukee,
cities and friends
I visited for a day
and began opened friendships
that will endure forever.

Washington, D.C. December 1981

Hebron Bus Stop

Barefoot children, beggars wearing
trashy scraps, shoddy kafiyehs,
shouting back and forth,
kowtow in our presence,
smile, flap hands, beg,
selling us their wares.
When we turn our backs
we hear uncouth, naughty words;
the brutal laughter, hate in their eyes,
send chills up and down my body,
make me dizzy with memories.
When stripped to the waist,
we were marched into prisons
to the tune of mad voices.
The tourists crowd,
return to our bus singing
Oseh Shalom Bimromav,
yet the children's raucous shoutings,
like a layer of dark smoke,
follow us on our journey
back to Jerusalem.
Silently I hear myself,
Hu Yaseh Shalom Aleynu. . . .

Jerusalem, November 1975

Mea Shearim

The truth is that
much against my will
I went to Mea Shearim;
I was embarrassed
by slogans on fences
equating Zionism with sin.

Still, coming from
a visit to Warsaw, Bucharest,
my soul was craving to see

an Eastern European Jewish
pattern of living
prevailing here as a way of life.
The streets, people,
the way they talk, walk, dress, —
a reminder of galut-diaspora.
Herzl, Bialik, Weizmann,
like the State of Israel, are
a cloud of evil here.

At an open window
a gray-bearded man is weaving
taleisim — prayer shawls.
A scribe writing a mezuzah,
voices of children learning Torah,
a beggar with a pushke, blind,
keeps repeating blessings every time
he hears someone passing by
dropping a coin in his box.

Heavy-hearted as I feel, my lips
bless the elders here who look
like Elyahu the Prophet,

The children: Moshelech, Shlomelech,
Chanelech, Sarahlech — my fortress
of strength and faith.

They are the guardians,
living witness of happiness, grief;
the future will make us One!

At the Foot of Mount Gilboa

At the foot of Mount Gilboa
I put a stone under my head
and took a nap. I dreamed
of Jacob's Ladder, armed P.L.O.
"ascending and descending on it,"
like the angels in the Holy Scriptures.
I was in combat with them,
trying to move upward to heaven.
I wanted to ask my Heavenly Father
to keep his promise and
"Bring us back into this land,
long enough were we the 'dust of the earth'. . . ."
But, the sun from Beth Shean
kept getting in my eyes,
heating the ladder steps with fire.
The stone I was resting on
did not like my dream and
burned my head.
A Japanese woke me with
unusual politeness, manners I was not
used to by the sons of ancient
Jacob and modern Israel.
"Come with me to Kibbutz Hefziba,"
he said in Hebrew.
"You will rest and renew
your dream. This land is
the gate of heaven."

I still wonder what was real:
My dream? or the Japanese
who spoke Hebrew?

        Kibbutz Hefziba, Israel

Sinai Dreams. . . .

Jethro's descendants
in Bedouin attire
sit on barren dunes
at the Mediterranean Sea.
A merciless sun
bakes the desert sand
and reminds us of
our forefathers' courage
leaving safe Goshen
to roam this wilderness
for forty years
on their way
to the Promised Land.
We, who traveled by bus
only seven hours,
are ready to call it quits.

The blue heaven and I
adore our reflection
in the clear ocean.
We are bursting with
excitement, jumping
against waves.
We rest in gray sand,
enjoy a sea breeze,
share food with our
distant cousins —
children of Bedouin nomads
who share with us
an ancient faith and appetite.
Together we stretch
on the sand and rest.
Dreams take on form:
I see this desert changed
into green fields, orchards,

villages full of people,
Arabs, Jews, together.
I see cruise ships, barges,
coming from Haifa, Cairo,
bringing tourists, traders,
guests on friendly visits. . . .

Yammit-Raphiah, November, 1975

On the Golan Heights

Then Moses separated three cities beyond the Jordan
towards the sunrising. . .and Golan in Bashan, for the
Manassites.
Deut. 4, 41-43.

A raven-haired young woman
with an open face like sunshine
greets us with a hearty Shalom.
She pushes a stroller with
twin infant girls smiling at us.
We ask her the way to the guest house
and she invites us to follow her.
The raven-haired, brown-eyed young woman
points to the playground, where children
and their teachers are romping together.

After refreshing ourselves in the
guest house, we stroll with the young woman
to the top of a concrete shelter.
She points to Lake Kinneret, glittering
in the sun. We see small fishing boats,
leisure cruisers sail the Biblical Sea.
The raven-haired young woman with lips
like dark cherries quietly explains:
"From this fortified bunker, the Syrians
shelled our settlements in the Valley."

"For nineteen years this bridgehead
kept up firing at our workers in the
field, causing us suffering and victims.
And here is our monument for the fallen
soldiers who stormed the Golan Heights.
You will find many like them everywhere
in our land. They are very dear to us.

"the Golan is an integral part of Israel;
we came here to work this land and
protect the settlers of the Hula Valley."

We walk around flower gardens, little
houses built of stone and concrete
like the shelter decorated with slogans:
"Anachnu Ve'atem — We and You, will make
the desert blossom." The young woman
with the raven hair and friendly smile
shows off their chicken coops, turkey
houses and their vegetable fields.
She also points out barbed wire, bunkers,
a watch tower. "We are on constant alert!"

When I hear people talk about the Golan,
I see a young woman with raven hair,
pushing a stroller with twin girls, I see
a slogan written on a shelter: "Anachnu Ve'atem —
We and You will make the desert blossom!"

On the Other Side of Sambatyon

For five decades I travelled the oceans
thrown from ship to boat by mishaps,
disasters, storms. I suffered pain, sorrow,
constant danger of being destroyed.
Still, I continued my venture, the journey
to the mysterious River Sambatyon.

I hoped to reach the Ten Lost Tribes,
to find them living in peace and harmony,
working their fields with their own hands,
spending their free time in song, dance,
delight in reading folk tales, composing
poetry and dreaming of the Third Temple.

After five decades on my journey to my
dreamed-of land, I reached the shores of
Sambatyon, greeted by the little Red Jews
throwing stones into my boat. . . .
They offend, dampen my spirit with ancient
laws. My Jewish credentials are in question.

For some of the Sambatyon spiritual leaders
I am not red enough to dwell in the land
of the little Red Jews. Five decades of hope
turn into misery. Prophet-dreamer Herzel:
What happened to our fellow Jews in our
beloved dreamland at the River Sambatyon?

Washington, D.C. September 1977

Second Class Citizens?

To Elton J. Kerness

I am possessed by a feeling of guilt.
My desire is not to exaggerate what
we saw, but to make perceptible to you
the tragic fate of some native Israelis
not integrated into the country's growth.

Iraqis, Moroccans, Tunisians, Yemenites,
walk aimlessly the streets of Lod, Bet Shemesh,
the alleys from Kiryat Sh'mona to Ashkelon.
They see Israel on the march forward,
their own lives full of frustration, fear.

Their parents, transplants from the Atlas Mountains,
Bagdad ghettos, Casablanca mellahs,
are old, sick, illiterate, living on relief work.
They are a Dor Hamidbar who will never change,
but their Sabra children worry and scare me.

Their shikuns look like Harlem dwellings;
many here still live six to a room,
children neglected by parents, uncared for by society.
The heat drives the youngsters out into the street;
they're asking: Why did you bring our parents here?

I look at able-bodied young men sitting here,
waiting for something to explode, to happen.
They feel that because of their Oriental background
someone is discriminating against them. WHO?...
Slogans — "We are One" — will not help here. Deeds will!

Kiryat Sh'mona, Nov. 1975

213

From Warsaw to Masada

To Zivia Lubetkin-Zuckerman

From the pits of Gensia cemetery
we climb brown rocks up to the cliff
of a gray fortress built by the Maccabees,
to the bare walls of Herod's Palace.
We whisper a silent Kedusha to Ben Yair
and the brave defenders of Masada,
the grandeur of martydom and resistance.

Historians search in vain for the remains
of nine hundred and six Zealots, men, women, children,
insurgents who withstood the Roman siege.
We have never discovered their bones and ashes,
but we have seen their spirit hover
over Ghettos Warsaw, Vilno, Bialystok,
spreading simple faith to the rebellion.

Menachem Ben-Yehuda spoke to the Jews of Poland
with the voice of Rabbi Menachem Zemba:
"I command you to learn how to defend yourselves
with arms. Do not surrender. Fight back! Take revenge!"
Elazar was the inspiring force for Malachi-Anilewicz,
Josephus Flavius's role was taken over by Ringelblum.
But Josephus was a deserter and Emanuel was a hero.

Here at the slopes of Masada, time stands still.
The Dead Sea, the desolate desert and Sdom
remind us of the remoteness and isolation
of Polish Jewry surrounded by silence
and indifference during the Holocaust.
We say Kaddish, sing "Am Yisroel Chai!"
and vow: Masada will never fall again!

Coexistence

A flaming sun
looks down from
behind Judean mountains,
A light wind
carries waves of hot dust,
rotated by a tractor
driven by an olive-skinned
half-naked man,
ploughing a stretch of field
at the barren roadside
in the Jordan Valley.
The dust settles on
a plastic strip
which covers his eggplant,
tomato and cucumber garden.
Two boys follow the tractor,
skillfully picking weeds
to the tune of Arab music
coming from a transistor.
We greet the man
and his olive-skinned children
with a friendly hand-wave,
though we can't hear what they say,
their smiles, extended hands,
speak to us responsively.
At the roadside
an old bearded man
attempts to pull
an overloaded jack-ass
to the roadway. He yells
at his poor animal,
looks at us with suspicion.
One of us tickles the donkey
in a sensitive place. . .
and she moves on with wild tempo.

A crack appears on the
old man's carved face, a smile
like a beam of light.
The donkey is pulling,
he keeps yelling: Allah is Great!
Salaam! Salaam! Salaam!. . .

Rav Turai Karl

To Sam Schweid

Karl, regiment commander
on a Golan Base,
hair mussed,
face sun-drenched,
eyes laughing,
a tall, muscular man,
halted our bus
with a smile,
a playful charm:
"Asur! Asur!"
He kept swinging
his arm: "Turn Back!"
As warm his words,
so cold his gaze.
We turned around,
back to Kfar S'zold.
Minutes after
we embarked for rest,
artillery fire
and planes came
from the West,
attacking Syrian Migs
in the sky.

Later, while resting
in a Kibbutz Gan
we heard the radio:
Casualties on the Golan,
Karl Hirsh, Rav Turai,
age twenty-four,
was hit in the head."

> November 9, 1972
> Ramat Magshimim.

217

The Sabbath After Auschwitz. . .

An autumn sun was shining brightly,
a blue sky surrounded the mountains,
Sabbath penetrated the wir with its sanctity,
Yet, he was incapable of feeling the spirit
of this holy day in the Holy City.

He felt a cold wind blowing inside him,
his mind was dulled with dark memories;
horror, persecution, gas-chambers, pain,
flashes of the past come back to haunt him;
the demonic place Auschwitz-Birkenau.

Three days ago he visited this pit of impurity,
his soul is still soaked in a flood of tears.
Now he sees throngs stride with pride,
greeting him with warmth and affection,
but his lips are sealed, his heart empty

The sun was shining breathlessly bright,
the gateway to the heavens was open, clear.
Aimlessly he wandered to The Wall.
He had no desire to pray, beg G-d for what?
Grief gnawed at his sanity, his tongue couldn't move.

He approached the mass of singing people,
touched the cold stones of THE WALL,
a torrent of pain burst from his eyes.
A gray-bearded man gazed sadly at his face,
a hand touched his shoulder affectionately:

"— There is a time for sorrow, time for joy,
Please, join me, be my Sabbath guest."
"— I'm no company for you, I just visited Auschwitz."
The bearded man displayed a number on his arm:
"— I was an inmate in Birkenau thirty years ago!"

218

"— My friend, I couldn't pray at The Wall". . .
"— My son" — the old man continued — "Look up,
See how the sun is shining brightly?
no wall, no curtain separates Jerusalem from G-d.
All that matters: we survived, destiny make us live!"

All the way back to his hotel room
he hummed a melody the old man sang
at his Sabbath table. Dark visions vanished,
faith became meaningful again,
He felt the warmth of Jerusalem's sun!

Tisha B'Av in Jerusalem

We climb an exotic path of narrow side streets,
centuries-old mud huts, stone houses lead us
to The Wall. We are overwhelmed by a large crowd,
equipped with prayer books, sitting on the ground
reading "Lamentations" with say voices, falling tears.

They remember Zion destroyed, exile to Babylon,
harsh years of captivity in Rome, the sufferings
our people endured through Nineteen Centuries. . .
I suddenly realize that I cry not from sadness
For I hear the voice of redemption in the "Eycha". . .

The redeemed are sitting right next to me
bursting forth with songs in many dialects;
I can hear the footsteps of the Messiah
in the banging of hammers, noise of drills,
building homes, schools, restoring Jerusalem.

With my ears I hear the lamentations of the past,
within my heart I feel happiness and joy, to be
with the exiles returned from lands of oppression,
the vision of the prophets are visible reality:
The city of despair is turning to cheerful glory!

Kibbutz Gonen

To Zivia Lubetkin o" h

A cool breeze descends from the Golan hills,
carrying a scent of tulips, fresh apples,
to the fields where young shepherds
guard grazing herds in the humid heat.

A young man with an Uzi on his knee
enjoys a pink, juicy pear. He greets us;
Shalom America'im! — Welcome Americans!
He offers apples, pears, a pitcher of water.
We ask: From where comes all this noise
which pierces our ears? Smilingly he responds:
"Our turkeys are holding a protest meeting
against the imminent visit of the shochet."

Sun-baked volunteers, bearded young adults,
girls in shorts, stand on hydraulic devices
picking apples, pears, working in the alfalfa fields,
talking in an amalgam of languages, dialects.

Their laughter blends with the voices of men,
carrying heavy bags on their strong shoulders,
tending fishponds full of carp, bass, pike,
and overwhelming the oasis with their song.

At the outdoor pool a blue-eyed girl
with a physique of a ballerina, thin, tall,
leads a class of children in gymnastics
to the tune of taped, classical music.

The fascinating view of the valley, mountains,
the panorama of the green fields, orchards,
the sound of conversation in Hebrew, between
an old man and a youngster on a ploughshare

Make me think of my life, my family, friends,
and, — G-d forgive me, — I feel jealous, trivial,
a miniature dwarf among tall, proud Jews. . .
I live with dreams; they make visions come true!

Safed

To Kathy Sokoly

An evening in Safed —
precious recollections
hidden away in the
storage cells of my mind.
Say Safed, and I hear a shofar blowing
from a mountain top,
sending signals to all Israel,
announcing the beginning
of a new moon during
the Second Temple period.

Chasidim, disciples of the Ba'al Shem,
Misnagdim, followers of the Vilna Gaon,
greet us with a Baruch Haba
as they welcomed pilgrims
in past generations, who traveled
thousands of miles
to this Galilean city.

We stopped to pray at the graves
of twenty-one children,
victims of the Ma'alot massacre.
While the Rabbi recited Aleynu,
chanted the customary Kaddish,
a child asked her father:
"Why?. . .They were so young!"
The sun was hiding her face
in shame behind the mountains.

That evening in our lodging place
all of us huddled together,
each pouring out his own feelings,
reciting his own prayers,
commemorating his own loss,
expressing his own joy,
for being able to be part
of the redemption of this land.

223

I was silent.
I kept looking at the faces
of my fellow Ole Regel — pilgrims —
and felt delight. My heart
recited Hallel Ha'gadol.

From the corner of the room,
reflections appeared in the mirror,
images resembling vividly
a likeness to two men:
Rabbi Joseph Caro — Ba'al Shulhan Arukh —
his face pale, ascetic, thin from fasting
Mondays and Thursdays, his beard gray
but his eyes burning with fire.
And Rabbi Isaac Luria — Founder of Kabbalah —
a smile of great satisfaction
was visible from the corners
of his mouth and the look of his eyes:
"I am proud and happy," Rabbi Caro said,
"that after generations,
centuries of catastrophes,
our people travel over oceans
to study my Code of Jewish Law,
practice charity and redemption."

Rabbi Isaac Luria smiled,
stroking gently his black, round beard;
"What contributed significantly
to this ecstatic outpouring of feelings
in this room tonight
was that the people experienced a revelation:
they affirmed their bond with ancestors,
with us, by seeing and listening
to a little girl revealing her soul.
They learned from a child what is love,
responsibility, honesty, loyalty.
They are now our messengers,
our foremost disciples.
Safed will forever live
in their conscience."

Facing Kunetra

The settlers here are mysteriously quiet
like the desolate volcanic mountain range;
their faces, hard like rock, evidence of
determination, character, idealism. They gave up
comfort, secure life-styles, for this lava soil,
danger of attack by Syrians, Al Fatah terrorists.

In the midst of the mountainous formation,
we hear music coming from a thriving Kibbutz,
children's voices echo in the hills: "Achad, shtayim,"
Green fields, planted crops, herds of sheep,
fishponds full of carp, playgrounds full of children,
tractors pull plowshares up to the border fence.

The young, mustached soldier with his Uzi — gun —
comes from Kibbutz Gonen, the valley below.
He goes by the Biblical name: Boaz. He will not
tell us his last name, yet he shares memories.
"We lived many years under Syrian guns, roads mined,
crops destroyed, shepherds slain, constant danger!

Here, the wind is piercing, nights bitter cold,
but our children in kibbutzim below are safer, warm.
This position on the Golan mountains facing Kunetra
is our security line for peace in the valley."
Down the road, a Druse fellahin, selling apples, calls:
"Salaam!" We replied:
"INSALLA — GOD WILLING, SHALOM-SHALOM."

From Hell to Hope

From a fretful visit to Poland and Rumania,
our plane is circling Ben-Gurion Airport.
Eagerly we peep through tiny windows,
see banners, slogans: We Are One! Welcome!

There is excitement in the tranquil terminal.
We are greeted cordially, like close family
who have come to visit kinfolks, to share,
feel, see how life is after Yom Kippur, 1973. . .

Lights are bright, faces look somber, solemn,
warfare is over, hostilities still go on.
On rooftops in all public buildings, schools,
armed guards are on alert, keep vigil. . .

At Mogen David Adom, Israelis, tourists,
line up to give blood, still in great need.
Soldiers with missing limbs, young, bold,
wait patiently in line at "Tel Hashomer."

While Chasidim dance at the Western Wall,
young widows, holding children, pour out grief,
beating with their fists the cold stones:
"Rebono Shel Olam! Why Me? Why Me?!". . .

A little girl is pulling at her mother's coat:
"Ima, tell Hashem how much we miss our Abba,
the war is over now, other fathers have returned,
ask Him Ima, when will my Abba come home?"

At Mt. Herzl, a man with a number on his arm,
prays at a grave bearing only numbers. He cries:
"G-d, How many akeydas do You want from me?
Four children lost in Chelmno . . . now this"

Shehecheyanu

"My vision of the future?
A Jewish state in which masses of Jews
from all over the world will continue
to settle and to build; an Israel bound
in a collaborative effort with its
neighbors on behalf of all the people
of this region; an Israel that remains
a flourishing democracy and a society
resting firmly on social justice and equality."
Golda Meir

For being able to visit Israel:
Cities, Kibbutzim, settlements,
From Rosh Pina to Yammit.
For the opportunity to pray,
To dance with new immigrants
At the Western Wall,
To cry at Yad Vashem, Ya'ar Herzl,
Rejoice on Yom Ha'atzma'ut at the Knesset,

For having known Chaim Weizmann,
Chaim Nachman Bialik, Ben Gurion,
Zalman Shazar and Golda,
For having witnessed the shaping of their ideals
Into reality: The transformation
Of 'Shaarit Hapleita' from lands of oppression
Into a nation living in dignity.
For the privilege of having lived
To participate in celebrating
Israel's Thirtieth Anniversary:
SHEHECHEYANU!

I was standing on the Golan
looking down on the splendor
of the valley below,
admiring the reflection of
the blue sky in the Kinneret,
the green fields and orchards
of the kibbutzim.

I lifted my eyes to the
heights of Mount Hermon,
inhaled the cool air
and said: Shehecheyanu.
From the mountain came an echo,
like the sound of blowing shofars
calling "Welcome."
The sound of wind and horns
mixed with the melody on my lips.
I felt a desire to sing —
to rupture the stillness
around me with a prayer:
Shehecheyanu.

BRACHELE

Brachale

Two Velvels

I was showered with love by my grandparents, pity and sympathy by my teachers; what I really needed was the affection and attention missing after my parents died.

I enjoyed being a student at "Yeshiva Beth Meir" in the town of Piotrkow Tribunalski, run by the Orthodox Agudas Israel. We were free to choose the *Talmud* tractates we liked to study and we learned Midrash, commentaries in Yiddish translation, but not in Hebrew; the "sacred tongue" was too holy to be used in daily conversations.

I was a pupil in "Machzikei Hadas Yeshiva" in the city of Lodz, Poland, and was transferred to Piotrkow Tribunalski to study until I would be ready for the "Seminary of the Lublin Scholars" founded by Rabbi R. Meir Shapira, of blessed memory, after whom our Yeshiva was named.

My teachers were mostly Chasidim — pious and learned rabbis. They were followers of the Rabbi of Ger, Rabbi Avraham Mordechai Alter, of blessed memory. I was fascinated by their sharp minds, humility and passion for learning. Many of them looked like my father, whose picture I kept in the table drawer in my attic room.

I was lonesome. I fell into a routine of talking to myself, arguing or singing in two voices. My imagination developed two separate and distinct characters. Sometimes we talked to each other, asking questions about *Gemara* and commentaries. We studied together *daf yomi* — a page a day of *Talmud*. We recited to each other pages of the *Mishna*, or chapters from *Pirkey Avos, The Ethics of the Fathers*, quizzing each other about who said what.

But one *Velvel* inside me was always creating friction; like a disciple of Satan, he argued with the pious disciple of the Gerer Rabbi. This other *Velvel* was overwhelmed by feelings of tension, irritated by the people in whose homes he ate free meals. These were compassionate people, gentle and curious Jewish mothers, or overgrown daughters, who served the food with a sigh, grieving over the "poor orphan." I felt smothered with so much pity that every spoonful of borscht they served was hard to swallow, and every morsel of bread stuck to my throat.

The first *Velvel* was a God-fearing student, sitting in the *Yeshiva* from morning till late evening. He showed competency and a degree of enthusiasm in his studies, to the satisfaction of his teachers. He was the delight of his grandparents, who dreamed their only grandson would be accepted to the great *Yeshiva* in Lublin.

The other *Velvel* in me had sinful dreams. He suffered feelings of inferiority for being so poor and so shabbily dressed. His shoes and clothes were falling apart at the seams. I was now going on seventeen, growing tall, and outgrowing my overcoat, which was too old, too tight, and missing many buttons.

"It is true," I argued with the other *Velvel*, "our rabbis don't care about *chitzionius* — exterior dress — the most important is *pnimius* — inner strength, willpower to study and do good deeds."

Both *Velvels* were lonely and homesick for my grandparents, whom we had not seen for more than a year. Last *Pesach*, I was ready to walk home to Lodz, but the weather was nasty and my shoes had holes.

The Twins

I had two days of two meals a day at the home of Reb Simcha the butcher. Leah, his wife, was possessed by a craving to do *mitzvot* — good deeds — to help others. She always carried small change for the poor.

They had two twin daughters, Feigele and Chanele. Both were good natured, always giggling, but fresh and aggressive. They always found a way, while serving my meals, to touch me, to lean on my shoulders so that I could feel their warm breath on my neck. They served my food as if they were stuffing geese before taking them to the ritual *shochet* slaughterer, always making remarks:

"*Velvel*, won't you come tonight and help me with my Yiddish lessons? I'll be nice to you . . . "

"*Velvele*, why don't you come and work for my father? You will have plenty to eat here, . . . We like you."

Little remarks like those gave me sleepless nights. I dreamed about the identical twin girls, laughing, leaning over my shoulders, their dark brown hair draping over me. I woke up bewildered, trembling, murmuring prayers, asking for God's forgiveness, and quoting Reb Yaakov: One hour spent in repentence and good deeds in this world is better (more exhilarating) than the whole life of the world to come. Yet one hour of satisfaction in the world to come is better than a whole life in this world."

But the other *Velvel* in me was happy with the dreams. They satisfied his desires. Such dreams were good substitutes for loneliness, supporting his cravings and longings for love.

The Kosher Inn

I spent two days in a kosher guest house. I helped serve meals from noon to two o'clock and in return I received a free meal and one zloty.

The waiters and waitresses kept saving leftovers for me — bread, pickles, sometimes a chicken leg or a piece of brisket. They wrapped the packages attaching little notes which I considered as temptations from Satan himself:

"Dear *Velvel*, you are as poor as we are. Quit wasting your life with the fanatics. We're all living in an uncertain future here. Join the Jewish Labor Movement, the BUND. Together, we will fight and build a better future for the Jewish masses of Poland. Take this note with the food to the other poor students of your *Yeshiva*. Come, join us. We need you!"

It was disturbing to receive this type of message. The girls and the men who worked at the Kosher Inn were all very nice to me and they never made fun of my earlocks. Just once, a young girl caressed my light chin whiskers saying: "Get rid of the earlocks and beard and I'll marry you tonight, even if you are only seventeen." Her remarks made me blush from ear to ear.

On my way back to the *Yeshiva*, I kept repeating: "Rabbi Yoshua ben Levi said: 'Eat bread with salt, drink water by measure, sleep on the bare ground, and live a life of hardship while you toil in the study of *Torah*. If you do this, happy shall you be in this world and in the world to come.'"

At the *Yeshiva*, I shared with my rabbi the conversation with the waiters at the inn. He said: "Worldly intellectualism, political movements, estrange our people from their heritage. Our *Torah* movement holds onto the principles of love of God and humanity. Your Reb Shmuel the Carpenter could draw near to our Heavenly Father as the *Tzadik* in his study in *Beth Hamidrash*. Your waiters are good-hearted people, but they came too late. Our *Torah* teaches justice for the poor."

My Attic Room

I lived in an attic room at the home of Reb Shmuel Isaac the carpenter. He was a devout Jew who inherited his father's carpenter's shop. The family business traced its mastery back to the seventeenth century, when the first Shmuel Isaac the carpenter helped build the famous Moses Kazin Synagogue in Nowa Wies, a suburb of Piotrkow.

The home was an old, one-story house with an attic converted into a room. Reb Shmuel Isaac's father renovated the century-old structure, adding a tall wooden fence, to keep out the noise and thieves. He also built a side door from the kitchen leading to the outhouse in the backyard. Reb Shmuel Isaac himself added a white-tiled oven with a chimney reaching high in the ceiling of my attic room.

The back porch had a sliding roof which could be moved back to show the sky. This was important for the celebration of the *Sukkoth* holiday. The *Sukkah* roof must be covered with pine branches and green leaves, but the stars must be visible through the roof.

Reb Shmuel Isaac was very proud of the fact that he managed to work from dawn to dusk, without forgetting to pray three times daily. He also attended evening study at his prayer-*shtibbl* and frequently visited his rabbi, the *Tzadik* of Ger.

While working in his shop, he often sang Chasidic melodies, recited psalms, and repeated chapters from *Ethics of the Fathers*. He always thanked Heaven that he was able to work with his hands. His work was creating foot stools, milking stools, rocking chairs, and doing furniture repairs in people's homes. Mostly he worked in his shop in the backyard of his house.

I felt a closeness to Reb Shmuel Isaac and his wife, Rebecca, from the moment I stepped into their house. He was a neat and gentle man, tall, with blond hair, and gray eyes. His small beard was trimmed and his rugged face was tanned from working outside. His eyes were red and ringed with dark bags from the heavy glasses he wore as protection from the sawdust in his shop. He wore a smile on his face that endeared him to his customers — Polish peasants and peddlers from nearby villages.

Rebecca, a shapely woman, wore a blond wig over her blond hair, had laughing blue eyes and talked with a melodious Warsaw accent. Rebecca helped run her husband's business, selling *"his creations,"* as she jokingly called them, at a stand in the market place.

Instead of paying rent, I helped Rebecca carry her wares every morning to the market and pick up orders for customers from shops or the apothecary, spices and dry fruits from Pinchas Tillis' food store, and kaiser rolls from the Toltsa Bake Shop. In exchange for these services, I received my attic room and breakfast every morning. I was also a "welcomed guest" at their *Shabbat* table if I so desired.

I enjoyed their hospitality from the moment I stepped into their house. On Friday nights the aroma of fresh baked *challa*, the sizzling *cholent* and *kugel* would waft from the oven and tickle my nostrils. The kettle of *Shabbat* tea was full, and we enjoyed singing *zmiroth* — Sabbath songs — all evening. It was good to be with them and they felt good having someone like me in their home.

They were lonely people, devoted to each other, with no close relatives or friends in town. Their only daughter, Brachale, was away. She graduated the Sarah Schnirer Teachers' Seminary in Cracow and was now teaching at a Beth Jacob School for Girls in Lodz. All letters to Brachale were written by me and dictated by Reb Shmuel Isaac or Rebecca.

Rebecca would awaken at the first sign of daylight and cook for the whole day. I helped her bring in the firewood from the shop and carried water from the well when the water-barrel was low, especially during the winter season. Sometimes, on his way home, a peasant would get drunk and Reb Shmuel Isaac would let him rest on one of the wagons in his yard. I helped feed and water their horses . . . .

At mealtimes they would ask me about my parents, my grandparents, what I wanted to be in life, how I was doing in my studies . . . There was no pity, no crying over me — the orphan. Repeatedly, they would ask me to read to them their letters from Brachale, and would show me pictures of her with her class of students. It was inscribed: "To my *Tateshi* and *Mameshi* from their loving daughter, Bracha." Thus did I become part of their lives.

≡ 2 ≡

Piotrkow Tribunalski

The provincial town of Piotrkow was the site of the General Assembly in prepartitioned Poland with a long history going back to the year 1578. It is located at the crossroads between Lodz and Warsaw, with good roadways connecting many of the small villages and farm communities. Jews played a role here in the struggle for independence and in the economical development of the area. They lived in harmony with the Poles for hundreds of years.

Market day was almost every day in Piotrkow and this kept Reb Shmuel Isaac and Rebecca very busy. Peasants with their horsedrawn wagons and coaches came directly to the shop or to the market stall, they traded farm products for milking stools and merchandise that Rebecca sold on consignment for small shop owners, such as barrels, pottery, brushes, kettles, saddler goods and other farm utensils. The farmers liked to deal with Rebecca. Often they asked her for advice in personal matters, and trusted her with orders for materials and merchandise to be picked up by them on the next market day.

The Polish peasants, themselves poor but very religious souls, shared their meager belongings with the less fortunate among them. The farmers always kept bundles of fruit, vegetables or home-made bread with them on the coaches and generously gave it to the beggars and poor at the market place. They also shared with the invalids who always sat on the steps of the parish church on Farna Street, and the Bernardine Monastery on Kosczuszko Square. They even rewarded me with fruit and vegetables when they saw me helping Rebecca pick up merchandise from the shops or apothecary. Naturally, I always shared the fruits with my rabbis and the other students.

Rebecca had her favorite customers and always greeted them with a little tobacco, a piece of egg-*challa*, honey cake or a bottle of *bimber* — vodka and wine, as little gifts of appreciation. After a while, the farmers knew that I was studying to be a *Rabin* and they would leave an extra egg, flower seeds or fruits for that "poor orphan."

And the two *Velvels* in me kept battling each other: Is this your future . . . ? Proclaiming to the world that you are an orphan? What will become of you?"

"I get paid for pick up and delivery of the farmers' orders. What's wrong with that? Thank God I don't have to carry back any merchandise in the evening." Actually this was more Rebecca's particular genius than my salesmanship. Rebecca knew exactly what would sell on a given day, as surely as her husband Reb Shmuel Isaac knew the exact prayers for sickness, rain, the evil eye and thanksgiving. "What could be wrong with earning some food as long as I did not neglect my studies?"

A World of My Own

At the Yeshiva I was in another world. Here both of my *Velvels* shared inner peace as we heard Rabbi Yaakov Yochiel explain *Mishna* or *Gemara* with a parable or tale. The same Rabbi Yaakov Yochiel told us moving narratives about the *Tzadikim* — saintly Rabbis of Kotsk and Ger, and brought us to ecstasy by the passion of his stories. He sang melodies of the Rabbi of Modzice, pouring out his heart to God *"Meshiach Zol Shoin Kumen"* — that the Messiah should finally come. Not only did he know "The Turim" and "Shulkhan Arukh" — books of Jewish law — by heart, he knew exactly where it was written and what were Rashi's and the Tosafists' comments on those passages.

Both *Velvels* loved and respected my rabbis for their humility and goodness, and for their scholarly minds. I felt delight just sitting there and listening to them — then unravel passages from "Maimonides" in such logical terms that a child in elementary school could understand.

When I was allowed to study on my own, I put my heart and soul into the books. I immersed myself in study, and the other *Velvel* in me, with all its desires, dreams, and complaints, had no entry here. This was a sacred place of Divine Spirit. Here my soul thirsted for God.

Dreams of Flesh and a World to Come

But the nights were terrible. Dreams . . . May God forgive me. Why is He teasing me? Girls . . . The Kosher Inn. Waitresses ten years older than I. The butcher's daughters, Feigele and Chanele. All of them in such perverse dreams. And lately, this Brachale. All I saw of her were pictures. All I knew of her were letters. All I knew of her was that she was a teacher at a girls' school in Lodz. She had been away from home for years now. She spent her vacations teaching in a summer camp in Bielsko-Biala.

From Brachale's letters which Rebecca would let me read I knew Brachale was engaged to be married to a student soon to receive *Smicha* — ordination as a rabbi at the Sfat Emet *Yeshiva* in Ger. I knew that they registered at the "Palestine Amt" in Warsaw for a permit — certificate — to go to Palestine and hoped to teach there at the General Orphans Home in Jerusalem. I knew in my mind that she belonged to someone else, still I dreamed about her. In my dreams I asked, "Why do you have to be three years older than I? Why don't you come home to visit your parents, you, their only child?"

Rebecca would sigh about how terribly lonely it was when Brachale left. "She was a bright student, always reading, studying and dreaming of being a teacher. Now, thank God, she is a

239

teacher and her groom, they say, no evil eye, is a giant in *Torah*. Hopefully, when they settle in *Eretz Yisroel*, we will follow. My Shmuel Isaac has a good trade, two golden hands, *kein eyin horo* (no evil eye), and they need carpenters everywhere," she would say.

But life went on. Rebecca kept herself busy with her customers and kept her home spotless. She baked bread, braided *chalah*, and made special honey cakes for her Brachale, who received the honey cakes by special messengers through merchants who had daughters also studying in Lodz.

Every Friday evening before greeting the Sabbath with the blessing over the candles, Rebecca would set aside small change for charity for the *Yeshiva* of Reb Meir the Miracle Man in the Holy Land. She also gave silver coins for the *Hachnasat Kallah* — the poor brides' fund of Piotrkow. She chanted her own special prayer in Yiddish for the poor people of the world; for her daughter, Brachale, and her groom Lazar — the scholar; for her husband, Shmuel Isaac; her customers; and her boarder, the orphan *Velvel* and *Kol Yisroel*.

> "May the Lord bless you and protect you;
> May the Lord raise his countenance upon
> you and be gracious unto you;
> May the Lord favor you and grant you
> peace."

Many times the other *Velvel* in me stood under the window before going to the *Shtibbl* to Sabbath services, just to listen to Rebecca's prayer, waiting to hear her mention, "My boarder, the orphan *Velvel* . . . ". Rebecca prayed with such sincerity that many times I cried.

As time went by and I progressed in my studies, I was able to spend more time helping Reb Shmuel Isaac and Rebecca. My life was divided now between the *Yeshiva*, my attic room, and the Kosher Inn where I still worked twice a week for two hours.

I was so immersed in study that an outside world did not exist for me. All I cared about was memorizing the commentaries of Rashi and the *Tosafot* explaining the laws and

240

Midrash reading. From morning to night I sat at long tables on hard wooden benches, singing out special melodies for chapter after chapter of *Mishne* and *Gemara*. My upper body rhythmically swaying back and forth to a melancholic, sweet sing song of "Omar Abayah — Abayah said . . . " Here, every day was Sabbath and on every Sabbath we were blessed with a Divine Spirit, an extra Sabbath soul.

Even on my way to work at the Kosher Inn, or while carrying the loads to the market following Rebecca and Reb Shmuel Isaac, the two *Velvels* in me argued back and forth about tractates in *Midrash*. We held a dialogue about the interpretation and commentary of the Bible, trying to solve problems, explaining meanings of words in the Babylonian or Jerusalem *Talmud*.

People on the street looked at me gesticulating, arguing with myself, humming a tone of a *Gemara* melody. Sometimes they would stop in astonishment and curiously look at my long, black coat, earlocks and fringes. But I paid them no heed. I went back to my *Tannaim* — the sages and teachers of the past. I did not care about the street or the outside world.

The only one who could disturb me was the other *Velvel*. He had such restlessness in him. "You don't care about the world you say . . . How about me? I am almost barefoot. Grandfather writes that grandmother is ill. How can you isolate yourself from everything? Is the *Yeshiva* the boundary of the universe? How about the demonstrations in the market place against pogroms in Palestine. Why aren't we part of it? The waiters at the Inn care about you. Do you care about them? What is our future going to be? Even if you get a scholarship to the Lublin *Yeshiva*, will you marry a girl and be supported by your father-in-law? We are living two thousand years in the past, in Babylonia, in the Temple of Jerusalem. We are studying laws of no meaning to present day life."

How could I allow the other *Velvel* in me to dominate my thoughts? I answered him reasonably. "What we are studying is for the future. We hold on to our traditions, to our laws from generation to generation. We see life constantly changing, but we continue to hold on to our sacred books, to our moral values, we hold on to our joys and sorrow, to our festivals and Sabbath, until the Messiah will come . . . ."

"The Messiah will come in a generation when all mankind will be guilty or righteous. With hunger, persecution and injustice in the world, the Annointed Redeemer is able to show up any day now — God willing. Stop your disputations, let's continue. Remember the Baal Shem Tov said: 'Do not mortify the flesh, pity it.'"

Longing

The Messiah did not come, but notes and letters from my grandfather in Lodz kept arriving. These were written in a beautiful Yiddish with Hebrew quotations. Letters full of love, that penetrated the heart and soul of both *Velvels*.

"Your *Bubeshi* — grandmother is ill. She feels guilty before our Heavenly Father and your mother's soul in heaven for letting you live so far away from us. She feels an unbearable longing to see you once more."

The "once more" was a shock to read. Heaven knows how much I wanted to help them, comfort them, be near them, and I was so helpless. What could a *Yeshiva* student do for them beside recite psalms and prayers? Both *Velvels* felt inadequate. Here I was, almost seventeen, at the level of self-study, and I could not figure out how to help the only people left in the world who were my family, my own. I clenched my fists at my own impotence. I was so helpless and ignorant of what was happening around me in the outside world. All I knew was *Olam Haba* — the world to come, but here reality intruded, the *Olam Hazeh* — this world. My grandparents.

Wait for the Messiah? According to my Rabbi Yaakov Yochiel, "There is a Messiah in every human being." He quoted the "Zohar" saying: "Redemption is not a thing that will take place at once at the end of the days; it is a continuous process, taking place every minute. Man's good deeds are single acts in the long drama of redemption. Redemption is not a process affecting merely the Jewish people; all the world is in need of redemption."

"All the world" — could it be that the Bundists and the Zionists are also part of the coming of the Messiah? Could it be the outside world has a part to play in redemption? Could it be that I am holding back the Redeemer by doing nothing but studying?

Piotrkow had a Jewish community with thirty *Talmud-Torahs* — Hebrew elementary schools, two Hebrew-Yiddish schools, an ORT (Rehabilitation through Training) School. It also had a Yiddish newsweekly. Maybe I could apply for a part-time *Melamed* — teacher's job? There were organizations from Agudas Israel and *Mizrachi* — Religious Zionist to Youth Groups like *Hashomer Hatzair, Gordonia* and *Zukunft*. There were *Kibbutzim* where young people, my age, learned trades, preparing themselves to go to Palestine. They worked in local lumber yards and textile factories. The *Bund* and Agudas Israel had summer camps and trade schools and they helped young men and women acquire skills and find jobs. Maybe they would be able to help me.

I felt inadequate and restless. What good is it that I know now the *Tannaim* — the sages of the *Mishna*, the sayings of Rabbi Yehuda Hanassi, the birthplaces of Abayah and Rava, the names of their cities in Babylonia, Pumpedita and Mahoza? How could I not know what takes place in the world around me? There is an enemy of the Jewish people named Hitler who is rising to power in the world. Can I fight him by fasting Mondays and Thursdays and reciting psalms? What good is all my study when on my own I don't know how to earn enough money for a pair of shoes, a decent coat, a clean shirt or my daily sustenance?

The two *Velvels* did not wrestle on this subject any more. We decided to find a new direction. We started to read, to look

243

outside at the world around us. It was a unanimous decision.

≡ 3 ≡
Brachale

One day, after the High Holidays, Brachale came home. While working in the summer camp in Bielsko-Biala, she became ill. She was bedridden all during the *Yom-Tovim* — the holidays. The doctor advised her school principal to send her home to recuperate for a few months.

I found her in the kitchen preparing lunch for her father.

"You are *Velvel*?"

"Yes, *Sholom aleichem*, Brachale. Welcome home!"

She greeted me with the familiarity of an older sister who had returned home. I knew she was three years older than I, but she looked younger than the picture in her room.

"Are you very *frum* — religious? Do you talk to girls? If you object, I will try not to bother or talk to you."

"Brachale, we were all waiting for you to come home."

"Me, too."

We all finished eating and said the final blessing. Reb Shmuel Isaac took some food to the market to Rebecca.

I was reluctant to say anything. I just watched her washing the dishes. Her light brown hair was woven into two braids and she wore them like a crown around her head. Her eyes were blue-gray with thick dark lashes. She was soft spoken, but firm.

"*Velvel*, what are your plans for the future?"

"I hope to study at the *Yeshiva* in Lublin."

"And then what?"

"Maybe I will go to Palestine. I have an aunt there."

"What is she doing in *Eretz Yisroel*?"

"She is draining swamps in the Valley of Jezreel."

Brachale looked at me with her blue-gray eyes and said, "*Velvel*, I don't know how many pages of the *Talmud* you can

recite by heart, but they will not help you dry swamps and re-
build the Jewish Homeland. It is very important to have a trade,
a profession. There are many Jewish organizations here that
will be able to help you. Our own Agudas Israel or ORT can
advise you as to what to do. Please go see them . . . will you?"

"I will. I was there already, but they told me to come back
next week."

"My *mamashi* told me all about you and I feel like I've
known you all my life from your letters. I don't want to get you
out of here, but honestly, I want to help you."

"Thank you. Isn't your groom a *Yeshiva* student?"

"Yes, he is. We hope to go to Palestine after our wedding,
God willing, and teach there."

I thanked her for the meal and the advice and went back to
my studies at the *Yeshiva*.

The following morning, the two *Velvels* started arguing.
One wanted to get up, wash his hands in the basin on the
washstand in the attic room and say his prayers. The other
Velvel was just lying in bed looking at the wall, observing a
spider spinning a web. He was full of envy:

"This spider is working, creating his nest. What is it that I
will do today? I am a parasite, just eating other people's food.
Brachale is right . . . What is my future going to be? Selling
mezzuzahs?"

"God will perform a miracle as he did with Elijah: He
ascended to heaven in a flaming chariot."

"Stupidity! How can you believe in all those stories you are
reading? These are fantasies, folklore, written by many people
in many different times!"

"Time to get up and pray."

"I am following Kotzk's tradition . . . spontaneity in
prayer, pray whenever the spirit moves you."

"Have you seen Brachale's delicate hands? Her voice is
. . ."

"She is someone else's bride."

"She is not married yet. What if her groom will not get

Smicha, will not graduate. Will she change her mind?"

Suddenly I heard Brachale's voice.

"*Velvel*? Good morning. Are you feeling well? It's late."

"I will be down in a few minutes."

I said my prayers, ran out of the house to the yard and followed Reb Shmuel Isaac with his merchandise loaded wagon to the market. I unloaded the hand wagon and helped Rebecca display the goods.

"*Velvel*, are you feeling well?"

"Yes, thank God. I just overslept."

ORT

The director in charge of the ORT School was tall and skinny with a clean shaven face and a head thick with black hair. He spoke Yiddish with a Lithuanian accent. He was polite, but serious. He offered me a chair and listened attentively to my answers to his questions.

"We have many *Chedorim* — elementary schools here. Would you like to be a *melamed*?" he asked, piercing me with his small sharp eyes.

"I'd rather learn a trade."

He gave me a brochure in Polish and Yiddish and a listing of trades I could learn locally, or I could be sent to an ORT School in Cracow, Lodz or Warsaw.

"At an ORT school you can learn to be a tailor, a meat cutter, a textile worker or a watch maker. Right here in Piotrkow. We have people in the lumber business who will teach you to be a carpenter or a lathe operator. All for free. Nevertheless, I advise you to go back to Lodz with the larger Jewish community and good schools. You have more opportunities there, but if for any reason you want to stay here, I will help you."

For some reason I was in no hurry to leave.

The Winter Season

Brachale was an avid reader of Hebrew, Polish and Yiddish books. She kept saying that every tongue people use in reading is a vehicle to better human relations. Languages spread ideas of good deeds and books bring inspiration and knowledge. The main object is to use wisely what we learn and read and to make good use of it in our daily lives. She did not object to my taking books to my attic room to read.

I swallowed her books with the thirst of a lost wanderer in the desert. I began to read and recite poems by Tuwim, Slonimski, Bialik, Peretz for the benefit of the other *Velvel*. I saved up a few zlotys and was able to send some *Chanukah Gelt* – Chanukah gift money to my grandparents. I was so proud of myself that for the first time in many years, I carried Reb Shmuel Isaac's milk stools to the market chanting loudly a Chasidic song the entire way.

"Hey you, crazy earlocks, what is it today? Purim?"

"Yes! I sent *Shalach-Mones* (Purim gifts) to my family."

I really was as happy as a Jew on Purim.

Winter came early that year. The old houses were buried under the snow. The streets were icy and dangerous.

The more I advanced in my studies, the more time I was allowed to study alone or at home. Because of the weather, many students did not come to the *Yeshiva*, but showed up only twice a week to be examined by our rabbis.

But, Heaven forgive me, instead of studying *Talmud*, I was reading books of Jewish history by Dubnow and Balaban; pamphlets by Max Nordau, Rabbi Zvi Kalisher; and books by Theodore Herzl, Borochow, and Ze'ev Jabotinski.

Every morning, after helping Reb Shmuel Isaac carry his creations to the market place, I helped Brachale carry wood from the yard to keep the fire going in the potbelly stove.

Rebecca came home exhausted in the evenings. After counting the daily earnings, she warmed her feet in a bucket of hot water and went to sleep.

Reb Shmuel Isaac returned home from evening services at his Gerer *Shtibbl* — prayer house. He ate his supper and went back to the shop to work until very late.

"This is the season when you must provide for the slow days in January and February," Reb Shmuel kept saying. "God will forgive me for not studying *Torah*. I will do it after Christmas when things get slower."

I would sit in my attic room reading books, writing to my grandparents, or just resting in the kitchen listening to Brachale.

Brachale was a good story teller. She loved her pupils and enjoyed teaching. She initiated and staged plays, dialogues with Biblical figures like Miriam, Deborah, Chana and her Seven Sons, and Queen Esther.

Her activities at school and at summer camp gave her great satisfaction and won her recognition. But she was too humble to speak about the awards she received. Her award was to see poor children from the lowest strata of society, lacking any kind of Jewish traditional background, turning to reading, learning, and becoming group leaders in the religious girls' movement. Brachale told astonishing stories about children and parents struggling for physical survival, living in terrible circumstances, in neighborhoods of crime, deprivation, and immorality. Some of the girls learned needlework, cooking, nursing; later, according to their talents, the school enabled them to learn various trades and sent them to *Eretz Yisroel*.

Brachale was soft spoken but bold with me: "Study of *Torah*, learning, and reading is very important for every young person, but with *Torah* must go *Kemach* — a trade, a vocation. You will gain respect when you will be able to provide for your daily needs." Both *Velvels* in me agreed with her and admired her honesty and straightforwardness.

My conversations with Brachale, her stories, her observations about people, books, *Eretz Yisroel*, were a great stimulation. In a short time I learned from her so much — I respected her as I did my rabbis. I was waiting already for the evenings to come to hear her voice calling: "*Velvele*, what are you doing upstairs?" Rapidly I came down to the kitchen.

Aches and Pains

One day in the week of Chanukah, Brachale returned home from the market place with a fever. Her face was as pale as porcelain, but her nose was red. She coughed and complained that everything hurt. Her hands were so icy that she wasn't able to remove her coat and galoshes. I helped her to the sofa.

"Would you like me to make some tea?"

She was shivering all over.

"I have painful cramps in my shoulders . . . Please, call my father."

I called Reb Shmuel Isaac and he helped Brachale to her room and put her to bed.

"*Velvel*, please stay downstairs. Brachale may call for something. A good rest and some tea will relieve the pain. I must finish an order for tomorrow morning. God help us."

Reb Shmuel Isaac started to recite prayers and psalms for her recovery and went back to his shop. I didn't need to be asked a second time. I felt the need to do something — anything to help.

Brachale called me. "I can't move my arms and ankles. I can hardly breathe . . . Everything hurts me."

"Shall I go and call Dr. Malewski?"

"Not now, it's snowing too hard. We will wait until morning."

In the meantime, I prepared some aspirin-powder with tea and lemon which she drank. Then I washed her forehead with a towel. Brachale was trembling.

"Where is my *mamashi*? My head is burning."

By the time Rebecca returned, Brachale was asleep. Rebecca watched her sleeping daughter and started to cry, "My

Brachale, the light of my eyes. I'd rather be sick than you." She did not count the daily intake nor did she eat. She just sat there on the old sofa, lamenting, praying, and finally falling asleep from exhaustion.

Growing Up

I remained awake all night at Brachale's bedside, adding wood to the stove, giving her tea, and changing the wet towel on her burning forehead. For the first time in my life I was taking care of somebody else. For the first time I was sitting so close to a young woman's bed. She kept pushing away the heavy feather quilt, uncovering her nightgown.

It was past midnight when Brachale awoke with severe cramps. She asked for her mother as she needed to go to the bathroom. But Rebecca was fast asleep so I assisted her. I covered her with her father's coat. She was holding onto me with her arm around my waist. I took her to the kitchen and sat her on the chamberpot covered with a special chair made by her father for use on cold winter nights. I left her and waited outside the kitchen until I heard her voice calling me. I took her back to her bed, covered her, and stayed near her. Listening to her rapid breathing was frightening to me. I added some wood to the stove and returned to her bedside. I felt the need to stay close. Maybe by sharing space I could also share my strength.

For some reason I was not tired. I watched Brachale shiver as if she was having convulsions. I was scared, but I felt stronger than Rebecca and Reb Shmuel Isaac. I felt like I was their stand-in, capable of protecting Brachale until morning, naturally, with God's help.

"Father in Heaven, please help her."

I looked at her feverish face and suddenly realized how dear this young woman was to me: how precious, how close, and also how dangerously ill, and I cried.

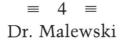

≡ 4 ≡
Dr. Malewski

Dr. Stanislaw Malewski lived only two small streets from Reb Shmuel Isaac, in a home hundreds of years old. He was a Pole born in Piotrkow in a family who had lived here for many generations. His forefathers were the founders of the Farna Church and Polish Patriots.

Everybody knew Dr. Malewski — the missionaries, the textile workers, the Jews, and the peasants from nearby communities. He was a short friendly man, with gray hair, a gray mustache and gray eyes. People greeted him with respect. Even orthodox Jews lifted their hats in reverence and respect to him. Many times, he helped the poor by providing them with money for medicines.

Dr. Malewski had known Reb Shmuel Isaac when he was still in short pants. He remembered his late father who left the Rabbinate to become a carpenter as had his father before him. Reb Shmuel Isaac did a lot of work in Dr. Malewski's old home. He built shelves for equipment, book cabinets, an examination table, desks and benches for the doctor's waiting room and a fence for his little yard.

When Dr. Malewski insisted that he pay for Reb Shmuel Isaac's services, Reb Shmuel Isaac resisted saying, "We are childhood friends, neighbors for a hundred years. You delivered my Brachale . . . Take money from you? Never!"

So Dr. Malewski, the most distinguished practitioner in Piotrkow, felt at home at the house of the humble carpenter.

Dr. Malewski came in the morning and locked himself in Brachale's room. He came out drying his hands on a white towel. His gray eyes looked sad. He knew the medical history of this family and did not inquire about possible inherited diseases. He spoke Yiddish as he stroked his grey hair and mustache.

"I can't give your Brachale a complete physical examination in her condition." His old, wrinkled face reflected his anguish. "Shmuel Isaac, I want to be as truthful and accurate as possible. I am afraid Brachale shows all the symptoms of pneumonia — inflammation of her lungs. I want you to bring me some of her stool and urine as soon as it is possible. Here are some powders to give her every two hours, and here is a prescription to be picked up immediately from the apothecary. Shmuel Isaac, you did the right thing by giving her aspirin and sponging her. Continue with the tea."

Reb Shmuel Isaac pointed at me saying, "He did all this, our *Velvel*."

"A relative?"

"No, a boarder, a student at the *Yeshiva*." Dr. Malewski studied my face for a minute before he said, "He will make a good *Feldcher*, a good medic. Give her plenty of liquid and keep sponging her. This helps keep the temperature down. I will come again to see her this evening. You, *Velvel*, when you're ready to take a job in a hospital, come to see me."

"Me in a hospital?"

"Why not? Isn't it God's command to help people in need? When you are in the apothecary, pick up a thermometer and a bed pan. Don't let Brachale out of bed until I say so."

I helped Dr. Malewski with his fur coat and opened the door for him. Reb Shmuel Isaac and Rebecca followed him to the door with thanks and blessings.

Convalescence

For four weeks while Brachale was ill, Dr. Malewski came to visit her almost daily. There were no beds available in the city hospital, so Dr. Malewski obtained a nurse and she rearranged Brachale's room into a miniature sick room. Even though it was cold, she insisted that the window be kept open for a few minutes for ventilation.

Reb Shmuel Isaac raised the bed with woodblocks to make it more convenient to feed Brachale. The sheets and pillow cases were changed daily. The floor was cleaned with carbolic acid.

At night, I frequently touched her lips with petroleum jelly because they were chapped from the fever. When I did, Brachale would hold onto my fingers.

Dr. Malewski ordered that I wear a face mask and a white gown when I fed her or rubbed her with alcohol or when I turned her from side to side to prevent bedsores. He would often tease me saying, "How is *Velvel* the 'doctor' today?" He brought medicines, home-made preserves and sometimes a real orange and juices in corked bottles with French writing on them.

Love Thy Neighbor

Rebecca neglected her business in the market place and asked her steady customers to come to the shop. The farmers brought chickens, butter, flour, winter fruits for "Brachale the Bride," and Brachale, on the advice of Dr. Malewski, drank milk with butter and honey.

I neglected my studies. I told my rabbis that there is sickness at the home of Reb Shmuel Isaac and they needed my help. My rabbis praised my charitable deed. They agreed that I was performing a great *mitzvah*.

Rabbi Yaakov Yochiel blessed me:

"The Almighty will reward you for helping a family in need, but I want you to take the Holy Books and study at home. God willing, when all is well, you will come in and we will examine what you've learned."

A New Vision

But one *Velvel* in me did not follow the Rabbi's advice. Instead of learning my discourses on the *Mishna*, the allegories of the *Midrash*, I was reading books published by the Polish Red Cross, pamphlets about home care, chronic diseases and first aid. Dr. Malewski urged that I read a book about communicable diseases and share my findings with Reb Shmuel Isaac and Rebecca, but not with Brachale. But how could I not share my new-found wisdom with Brachale?

New words became part of my vocabulary — bacteria, germs, strep infections. As Dr. Malewski ate a piece of honey cake dipped in Passover Wishniak liquor, he explained to me the difference between bacilli and spirilla bacteria.

A new world opened for me in the medical texts and magazines. I gorged myself with books. The trouble was that Brachale was also reading the books that Dr. Malewski left for me. From the books and her own good sense Brachale soon realized that she did not have the necessary resistance to ward off pneumonia. Her groom kept sending good wishes for a speedy recovery from the Rabbi of Ger. Reb Shmuel Isaac was delighted with the beautiful letters from his future son-in-law. But Brachale was having pains in her lungs and chest.

Brachale smiled for the benefit of her mother and father, but she walked around the house like a shadow, sad and quiet. She had a difficult time getting adjusted to being served. She was used to serving and helping others. She was anxious to get well and continue her plans to leave for Palestine. As the day of her wedding came closer, Dr. Malewski still did not allow her to do such things as visiting her school or her future in-laws. Dr. Malewski forbade her to even talk about it.

"You think you're well, Brachale, but a coach ride to Lodz is very tiring. I am talking to you not like a doctor to his patient, but like a friend. You are not ready yet."

One day I heard her asking Dr. Malewski the difficult question, "*Panie Doctorze*, do I have tuberculosis?"

"Unfortunately, Brachale, I must say yes."

"Will I be able to get married this year and leave for Palestine?"

"No, my child. I would rather advise you to go to a sanitarium in Otwock."

"Will I ever be able to get married and have a family?"

"Fortunately, we detected your disease early enough to hope you will fully recover. There are new drugs available. I'll start you on them as soon as they arrive. Plenty of fresh air and a lot of milk will also help you."

"Dr. Malewski, you are avoiding my question. Will I be able to get married this summer?"

"No, Brachale. A change in climate, plenty of rest and you will . . . "

"Forgive me, Dr. Malewski." Brachale ran out of the room sobbing.

Dr. Malewski looked after her sadly. I helped him with his coat.

"*Velvel*, do not leave her alone today and let me know tonight how she is. Sometimes it hurts, but I believe in telling my patients the truth."

The next morning, Brachale wrote a long letter to her groom and enclosed the *Tnaim* — the engagement contract.

"You are free from the "word of honor" we gave each other at our *Tnaim*. You are free to go to *Eretz Yisroel*. My blessings and good wishes go with you. The Almighty destined otherwise for me. Please, pray for my body and soul. Bracha."

≡ 5 ≡
Low Spirits

The task fell on me to get Brachale out of her room to eat or drink something. Reb Shmuel Isaac swallowed tears and recited psalms. Rebecca talked to the customers, scrubbed, cleaned and cooked. She did not realize the extreme depression Brachale felt about her condition.

Dr. Malewski said that millions of people in Poland have

lung trouble and are cured. It just takes time. "Brachale, have confidence in God. He will help. The Rabbi of Ger himself prays for you."

Brachale just sat there in her room, with no expression on her face, not even a nod. She had no tears for herself.

"*Velvel*, please leave me alone," she said quietly.

I had no desire to read or study or even to say my evening prayers that day. All I could think of was Brachale sitting in her room, motionless, and suffering. I asked myself what I could do for her now.

"I am only seventeen and Brachale is twenty. She is so much more aware of life than I am. But how can I just be here in this house and know she hasn't eaten or drunk anything since Dr. Malewski left?"

The other *Velvel* crept into my thoughts:

"For weeks now, I've been praying for her recovery. Her father, the Rabbi of Ger, the rabbis and students of his *Yeshiva* . . . why did God not answer our prayers? She is a pious girl. She wanted to give her life for *Am Yisroel* — to the teaching of Torah to orphans in the Holy Land. Why does He punish her? Her parents are God-loving, honest people. Why were they chosen for such suffering?"

"You blasphemer! How dare you ask questions like these? God, blessed be His name, will punish you for this . . . Remember what the *Gemara* in Sanhedrin says: 'And he that blasphemes the name of the Lord shall surely be put to death.' You recall it?"

"All I did is ask a question . . . "

"You must have more faith, just simple faith, 'Love God and have faith in Him.'"

Quietly I opened the door to Brachale's room. She was stretched out on her bed. Her face was pale, her eyes were half closed.

"Brachale, can I come in?"

"Please, *Velvel*, sit here," she whispered. "*Velvel*, did I ever tell you how I met my chosen — my Lazar?"

"No, Brachale, you did not."

"Would you like to hear?"

"Yes, very much."

"I have a girlfriend in our seminary, Goldie. Her father is a rabbi in Pabianice. One day, she invited me for *Shabbos* to her house and there he was, Lazar, her oldest brother. He was coming home from *Shtibbl*. He was tall and handsome, with dark eyes, long earlocks and a small black beard. Goldie arranged the seating at the table so that we faced each other. I knew she contrived this with the knowledge of her parents and the Dean of our seminary. He made *Kiddush* — the prayer over the wine, and we all sang *Zmiroth* between courses. There were many people at the Sabbath table, a house full of children, a poor wanderer — an *orach* they brought home for the Sabbath feast. I did not see anyone but Lazar. I was hynotized by his looks, fascinated by his voice. That night, for the first time in my life, I dreamed about a man holding me in his arms and the man was Lazar. I was ashamed and felt sinful for having this dream, but I was happy.

"The next morning I spent more time looking at myself in the mirror, trying to fix my braids more perfectly than ever before. After the *Shabbat Tzimmis* — meat with plums and carrots, dessert and grace, Lazar asked Goldie and me to stay at the table while his parents and the children left the room. Lazar talked to us looking at his sister:

"'Goldie, our rabbi brought his brother here, the Rabbi of Pabianice. He asked us, a group of students, if we are willing to go and teach in *Eretz Yisroel* at the General Orphan Home in Jerusalem.' He pretended not to notice my reaction and continued. 'Maybe you and some of your seminary graduates would like to consider going?'

"Lazar moved his black velvet skullcap back, touched his earlocks and turned his eyes toward me.

"'I am an only daughter. I don't know if I will be doing the right thing, leaving them. But, if our rabbi, be he blessed, asks us to go . . . Still, I must first ask my parents.'

257

"'Naturally.'

"'I don't believe my father will let me go, even with our rabbi's blessing . . . Not as a single girl.'

"'Naturally. There are good students in our *Yeshiva* who would feel honored to have you or Goldie for a wife.'

"I felt my pale face start to blush and the room became warm. Goldie kept silent. She did not utter a word. Lazar continued talking in a slow, awkward voice:

"'The Rabbi of Pabianice feels that I too should get married before leaving for Jerusalem, but not before I have *Smicha*.'

"He sat for a few minutes, looking at Goldie and me, then stood up. 'Please, think about it. It is a great *mitzvah* to help orphans and to go to *Eretz Yisroel*.'

"Lazar went back to Ger to study. Two months later I was engaged. We saw each other only four times at his parents' home, and once at the seminary where he came with another student to visit Goldie.

"Lazar took care of all the details — applications to the Palestine Agency for a certificate, permit to enter Palestine. We wrote to each other twice a week; I have all his letters . . . until this shock . . ." Brachale started to cry. "I am not strong enough to face it." Her trembling hand reached for mine. "God, what am I doing to my poor parents?"

"Dr. Malewski said they now have new drugs and with proper treatment, you can be cured."

"Not enough to go to Palestine with my Lazar."

"Maybe it is God's will that you should stay here with your parents. They love you so much. Your mother cries all day. You did not take your medicine and you did not eat. She is so unhappy."

"I am so selfish. All I was thinking about was of my magnificent future with my Lazar in Jerusalem. Now everything has collapsed. Oh, *Velvel*, I don't know which pain is worse. It is impossible to describe how I feel. The training in the seminary was hard and I prepared myself for service to our people, now . . . I can't even go near children. What is the purpose of living?"

"Struggle and hope, Brachale, for your parents' sake, for your own sake, and for mine." I almost choked on that last word. Brachale, still holding my hand, turned her face to me like seeing someone for the first time.

"Brachale," I continued, "My life was wrapped in a fog. All I knew was God, the rabbi and my studies. You, Brachale, made me see reality and distance, tomorrow, things my eyes could not see . . . "

Brachale listened avidly to what I said, took my hand and pressed it against her cold cheek. "*Velvel*, I wish you . . . " and she stopped. "Would you please give me some water. I want to take my medicine."

Shattered Dreams

Reb Shmuel Isaac and Rebecca insisted that I no longer sleep in the attic so I moved, and slept instead on a folding bed in the living room.

Rebecca, sick from aggravation and "God's punishment" was not able to attend to the business any longer. She stayed in the house, took care of Brachale and cried in the corners. I gave up study in the *Yeshiva*, my days at the Kosher Inn and at the butcher's. I now worked full time with Reb Shmuel Isaac in his shop. He himself spent less time now in the *Shtibbl* and devoted more time to his shop and his family.

Since the yard bordered on the heavy wall of the Bernardine Seminary, Reb Shmuel Isaac asked the Priest for permission to build shelves and a stand leaning against the seminary wall. In exchange, Reb Shmuel Isaac agreed to fix all broken pews and old doors in the century-old church. The farmers and small shop owners now came to order and buy the merchandise displayed on the wall-shelves.

Brachale and her parents insisted that they pay me a regular salary. I was reluctant to take any money from them, but

Brachale insisted that I take it. I bought new shoes, shirts, and socks, a real woolen sweater and an overcoat. I had to show off my new clothes for Brachale and for the first time in many weeks, I saw a gleam in her eyes and a smile on her face.

The week before *Pesach*, Dr. Malewski, this doctor of great heart came with the news that he arranged for Brachale to go to a sanitarium in Otwock. She had to leave the day after Passover.

I was also planning a Passover departure for myself. I started packing my belongings in a wooden suitcase made especially for me by Reb Shmuel Isaac. I said goodbye to Reb Simcha the Butcher and his family, and to the inn-keeper and the waiters at the Inn. I also said goodbye to my beloved rabbis and the students at the *Yeshiva* and to Dr. Malewski. They all gave me gifts for my grandparents and books for me.

After evening services, I spent my last evening with my rabbi, Reb Yaakov Yochiel. He spoke of ethical conduct, fear of God, the importance of honesty, indulgence in good deeds, prayer and learning *Torah*: "Constant study is the most important thing in life."

I sat near him answering questions. The other *Velvel* in me was just praying for Brachale: "O, please God, restore her health. Make her dreams come true."

Reb Yaakov Yochiel blessed me. He sent greetings and a blessing for my grandparents and gave me a sealed letter of praise.

Two days before *Pesach* I said goodbye and kissed Reb Shmuel Isaac and Rebecca. I kissed the *mezzuzah* on their door and went to the Piotrkow market place. I got a seat on a coach ready to leave for Lodz.

Brachale insisted on coming to see me off. She walked near me holding on to my arm. She was still very weak.

I was afraid to look at her face. I did not want her to see my tears. We walked without saying a single word, and the silence thundered in my ears.

When the driver was ready to leave, Brachale looked at me with her unnaturally big, tearful eyes and said, "*Velvele*, please write to me. Have a good kosher *Pesach*. I . . . I will pray for you . . . always."

I could not speak, but the tears were running down my face. Brachale wiped them off with her fingers. She leaned forward and kissed me on my cheek. Now both *Velvels* shared the understanding of how much Brachale really meant.

The driver hit the horses with his whip. I sat in the coach looking at Brachale's figure growing smaller and finally disappearing behind the old houses of Tribunalski Square.

Both *Velvels* prayed, "Heavenly Father, please watch over her and restore her health," and wondered if we would ever see her again.

This was the last I saw Brachale. We did write to each other until the summer of 1939. I went off to war and the Jews of Piotrkow perished in Treblinka.

Dr. Malewski survived the war and did write to me until just before he died in 1956. From Dr. Malewski I found out that Brachale and her mother were sent to Chelmno concentration camp. Reb Shmuel the Carpenter was employed at the Bugaj Timberworks until the liquidation of the Piotrkow ghetto.

◆ ◆ ◆

To the children
from Lidice, Czechoslovakia and from the Zamosc region
who were murdered with Brachale at Chelmno.
In a lasting memorial.